Marks of the
Missional Church

Marks of the Missional Church

Ecclesial Practices for the Sake of the World

Libby Tedder Hugus

Keith Schwanz

Jason Veach

Storian Press
Overland Park, Kansas

Storian Press LLC
PO Box 27112
Overland Park, KS 66225-7112
www.StorianPress.com

Cover designer: Christian Cardona of Krixel Diseño Grafico

Typesetter: Keith Schwanz

Copyeditor: Kevin G. Smith

Cataloger: Jennifer Steinford

Publisher's Cataloging-in-Publication Data

Tedder Hugus, Libby

Marks of the Missional Church: Ecclesial Practices for the Sake of the World / by Libby Tedder Hugus, Keith Schwanz, and Jason Veach / Storian Press, 2014.

185 p.; 23 cm. Includes bibliographical references.

ISBN 978-1-940402-02-4 (paperback); 978-1-940402-03-1 (ebook)

1. Church - Marks. 2. Mission of the Church. 3. Church Renewal. I. Schwanz, Keith. II. Veach, Jason.

BV601 .T94 2014

Library of Congress Control Number: 2014931533

Contents

Preface

WE BEGIN WITH A BENEDICTION:

Now to him who by the power at work within us is able to accomplish abundantly far more than all we can ask or imagine, to him be glory in the church and in Christ Jesus to all generations, forever and ever. Amen (Eph. 3:20–21).

We add our own *amen* to Paul's blessing to the congregation in Ephesus. We fervently desire a *so be it* for the church in the twenty-first century as it was for Paul in the first century.

In verses preceding the benediction (Eph. 3:16–19), Paul prayed that the congregation would "be strengthened in [their] inner being with power through his Spirit."

We say *amen.*

Paul ardently longed "that Christ may dwell in [their] hearts through faith."

Amen.

Paul wanted the congregation to be "rooted and grounded in love" and to know all of love's "breadth and length and height and depth."

Amen.

Paul prayed that the congregation would be "filled with all the fullness of God."

Make it so, Lord.

We wrote *Marks of the Missional Church* with the prayer that this book might be a means of grace to strengthen the church. We hope missional communities find guidance as they seek to discern God's redemptive work in the world. We hope that insights prompt courageous acts as missional communities align their practices with God's mission. We look forward to God's glory emanating ever brighter in the church.

We have used three terms in specific ways in contrast to how they are sometimes used interchangeably. *Missional communities* is the term we use to describe particular expressions of those participating in God's mission. A missional community might be a traditional *congregation*, or a group within a congregation, or a group that exists in a non-traditional form. We reserve the use of the word *church* to refer to the whole of God's people.

Introductory Chapters

We begin by looking at the similarities between the congregations in Antioch and Jerusalem as described in the book of Acts. In chapter 1 we identify three insights that form the foundation on which the book is constructed. First, God molded a new community infused with the power of the Spirit. Second, the believers intentionally employed specific spiritual disciplines that formed the community in Christlikeness and facilitated its witness of God's grace. Third, the very fact that God had fashioned and empowered the church gave witness to the redemptive nature of God's mission.

Chapter 2 discusses how missional communities in our day intentionally engage in ecclesial practices as participants in God's mission. The emphasis in this chapter is the alignment of theological convictions with the words and actions of the church.

Chapter 3 unpacks the rationale for the structure of the book. A creed is a concise way to state doctrinal truth. We structured this book around the four marks of the church in the Nicene Creed — apostolic, catholic, holy, one. In chapter 3 we discuss why we reversed the order.

The first three chapters explore the underlying principles used in creating the main part of the book. While we think that readers will benefit by reading these chapters, we also recognize that in a group study some might find it preferable to begin with chapter 4. In this case, the group leader might summarize key ideas at the beginning of the group study.

Four Marks of the Church

The four parts following the introduction correspond with the Nicene marks. Each part begins with a theological reflection on the mark and an introduction to the three ecclesial practices discussed in that part of the book.

The chapters on the ecclesial practices begin with a contemporary story that shows an expression of that practice in a particular context. The theological rationale for the ecclesial practice is explored and used to reflect on current expressions of the practice and to suggest new or renewed ecclesial practices that embody the theological convictions.

Because of the goal of the book, in the stories we emphasize practices of the missional community and mention the leadership of specific persons as necessary to tell the story. We do not intend to minimize the importance of pastoral leadership — we have given our lives to serve God through pastoral ministry — but in this book our focus is on the body of Christ. We use first names of the persons involved in the stories. More detail about the persons, congregations, and missional communities referred to can be found in the back of the book.

In every chapter about the four marks of the church and the ecclesial practices, we offer a collect and a benediction. We intentionally utilize these corporate worship forms because we understand the ecclesial practices we propose as an act of worship. Through these ecclesial practices we respond to God with lives that embody our praise and thanksgiving.

A collect (KAHL-ekt) is a compact prayer structure that begins by articulating an attribute of God before taking a turn to a petition for God to act in character. Consider the often-used collect for purity as an example. The prayer begins with a description of the all-knowing God:

> *Almighty God, to whom all hearts are open, all desires known, and from whom no secrets are hidden:*

Then the collect makes the turn toward the petition for divine action:

> *cleanse the thoughts of our hearts by the inspiration of your Holy Spirit,*

This request is followed by the reason for the petition:

> *that we may perfectly love you, and worthily magnify your holy name;*

The collect closes with a statement of mediation, as in this example, or an ascription of praise:

> *through Christ our Lord. Amen.*

We created the collects in this book with the readers in mind even before we completed the manuscript. The petitions emerged in concert with the drafts of each chapter.

We conclude the chapters with a benediction. Unlike a collect or prayer that is spoken to God, a benediction is addressed to God's people. At the end of a worship service, for example, the pastor blesses the congregation. The Aaronic blessing says:

> *The Lord bless you and keep you; the Lord make his face to shine upon you, and be gracious to you; the Lord lift up his countenance upon you, and give you peace (Num. 6:24–26).*

We ask for God's blessing on all who read this book.

The phrase *lex orandi, lex credendi, lex vivendi* reminds us that prayer influences belief that guides the way we live, and the way we live informs what we believe and how we pray. We hope this book stirs the imagination of your missional community so that its daily and weekly rhythm comes into better alignment with what God is doing in the world. May your missional community demonstrate the love and grace of God through its actions and testify to the good Word who lived among us to reveal God's glory.

Part I

Introduction

The church participates in God's mission by proclaiming to the whole world — all classes and cultures, all ages and genders, all nationalities and races — that God is holy love and, through Jesus, God is transforming a people who embody that holy love as empowered and knit together by the Holy Spirit, a sign that the kingdom of God is here.

Nicene Creed

We believe in one God, the Father, the Almighty, maker of heaven and earth, of all that is, seen and unseen.

We believe in one Lord, Jesus Christ, the only Son of God, eternally begotten of the Father, God from God, Light from Light, true God from true God, begotten, not made, of one Being with the Father. Through him all things were made. For us and for our salvation he came down from heaven: by the power of the Holy Spirit he became incarnate from the Virgin Mary, and was made man. For our sake he was crucified under Pontius Pilate; he suffered death and was buried. On the third day he rose again in accordance with the Scriptures; he ascended into heaven and is seated at the right hand of the Father. He will come again in glory to judge the living and the dead, and his kingdom will have no end.

We believe in the Holy Spirit, the Lord, the giver of life, who proceeds from the Father [and the Son]. With the Father and the Son he is worshiped and glorified. He has spoken through the Prophets.

*We believe in **one**, **holy**, **catholic**, and **apostolic** church. We acknowledge one baptism for the forgiveness of sins. We look for the resurrection of the dead, and the life of the world to come.*

Chapter 1

Early Church Practices

Engagement in God's Story

PETER AND JOHN, AS JESUS' DISCIPLES, CONTINUED MANY OF THE Hebraic spiritual practices, including prayer at the temple in the middle of the afternoon. Other followers of Jesus joined them in this practice.

On one particular afternoon, as they made their way through the court of the Gentiles, a lame man called out to them for a coin or two. Every day, friends carried this man to this place. He lay on the stone courtyard hoping that those who walked to worship would find their hearts softened and their hands generous.

The apostles might have merely walked by; they did not have coins to share. But Peter stopped right in front of the man. The man looked up as Peter said, "In the name of Jesus Christ of Nazareth, stand up and walk" (Acts 3:6). Peter's words were less a command and more an invocation to God and an invitation to the man.

Peter's actions matched his words when he reached down to grasp the right hand of the man. The lame man responded to the touch. He stood. He began to walk. Then he started leaping and shouting praise to God.

A gasp like an ocean wave swept across the crowd in the court-yard. They recognized this man and immediately knew something spectacular had occurred.

When the crowd rushed to get a better look, the formerly lame man clung tightly to Peter and John. For years he had watched people keep their distance while he sat on the pavement. Now they pressed in to get as close as possible.

Peter noticed a different attitude directed toward him, too. People looked at him like he had divine powers. He quickly redirected the attention and disowned any notion of personal power or piety that could bring healing. Peter repeated to the crowd what he said to the man — that wholeness came in the name of Jesus. He called the people to turn to the God through whom "all the families of the earth shall be blessed" (Acts 3:25). Thousands of people accepted the invitation that day.

The leaping and shouting of the man and the surge of the crowd attracted the attention of temple authorities. The captain of the temple guard and his entourage descended on those listening to Peter's sermon. The commotion annoyed the religious leaders. The sermon alarmed them. Everything that challenged the status quo had to be squelched immediately. Since sundown loomed on the horizon and with laws against night trials, the temple guard escorted Peter, John, and the formerly lame man to a secured place for the night.

An august body convened the next morning for the interrogation. Temple rulers, respected men from the community, and experts in the law joined the high priest to confront the ones who instigated the disruption. "By what power or by what name did you do this?" (Acts 4:7). Peter replied, "The name of Jesus Christ of Nazareth. . . . There is salvation in no one else, for there is no other name under heaven given among mortals by which we must be saved" (Acts 4:10, 12).

Peter made a deep impression on the authorities. A common man stood without chagrin before the wealthy. An unschooled man lectured the intellectuals. A man with no social standing confronted the powerful. Without the benefit of refined oratory skills, Peter addressed the elite with confidence.

Since the healed man stood next to Peter and John, the temple rulers could not refute that something notable had occurred. The crowds who caused the commotion in the temple courts would attest to that. But still, the authorities had to prevent this type of disruption from happening again.

After a private session, the temple leaders threatened Peter and John. The two pushed back. They pledged to respond to the threats with civil disobedience and disregard the command to stop speaking in Jesus' name. So the authorities threatened the apostles again, and then released them.

Peter and John hurried to where their friends gathered. They filled in the details about the previous day's experiences. The spontaneous response of the followers of Christ was to pray. They prayed for faithfulness to Christ and not vindication. They prayed for boldness and not eradication of their fears. They prayed as servants of the Anointed One and not as an entitled people. "And they were all filled with the Holy Spirit and spoke the word of God with boldness" (Acts 4:31).

Reflection on stories like this demonstrates that when life brings experiences that cannot be explained in usual ways, persons gravitate toward familiar habits. When crises come with roadblocks and threats, the natural inclination is to reset to the default position.

For the early Christians, foundational practices in difficult times included gathering as the community of Jesus followers, engaging in practices that strengthened their faith, and testifying of the God at work among them. When released from the custody of the temple guard, Peter and John went to be with their friends, they prayed, and they served as witnesses of God's powerful presence.

A Tale of Two Cities

When adverse reaction to the early church escalated in Jerusalem, especially following the stoning death of Stephen, Christians could no longer safely live there. They became seeds of the gospel blown by the winds of persecution.

As the gospel put down roots in Antioch, more than 300 miles north of Jerusalem, that congregation exhibited similar characteristics of the congregation in Jerusalem. The DNA of the Christians formed by direct interaction with Jesus and tempered by the fire of the Spirit migrated from Jerusalem to Antioch.

Christians in Antioch gathered as a community of Jesus follow-ers. The congregation in Antioch took on a multicultural character from the very beginning. The first ambassadors of Christ came from Cyprus and Cyrene and witnessed of Jesus to the Hellenists in Antioch. Leaders in Antioch came from a variety of backgrounds and cultural contexts. The new community that God assembled in Antioch breached the barriers often erected by cultural and religious distinctions.

This new group of Christ followers quickly became distinct from the culture around them. Old terms could not adequately describe this new group, so they devised a new term — Christian. What probably started as a word of mockery and ridicule proved to be fitting since it accurately identified the church as followers of Jesus Christ.

In both cities, the church practiced basic disciplines of the faith. Just as the congregation in Jerusalem attended to the apostles' teaching, so the believers in Antioch explored the Scriptures. After Barnabas witnessed the grace of God at work within this new community, he went to Tarsus in search of Saul. For an entire year, Barnabas and Saul taught the new Christians in Antioch. In both Jerusalem and Antioch, the Scriptures played a dominant role in nurturing the believers in the faith.

The Antiochian congregation engaged in prayer just as their brothers and sisters in Jerusalem did. This practice resulted in significant initiatives. While the believers in Antioch prayed, the community recognized God's will that Barnabas and Saul be sanctified or set apart for the apostolic mission of taking the gos-pel to those who had yet to hear the good news. God shaped the Christians in both Jerusalem and Antioch as the believers listened to God through the Scriptures and prayer.

The *koinonia* or "fellowship" of these congregations had a cen-trifugal spin that compelled them to use their resources for the benefit of those in need. In Jerusalem, no person remained needy very long. In Antioch, the Christians responded generously during a severe global famine.

In both cities the early Christians told the story of Jesus. The early church in Jerusalem often proclaimed the resurrection of

18

Jesus. Likewise, those who brought the gospel to Antioch proclaimed Jesus as Lord. Jesus formed the content of their message. Jesus shaped the character of the community. Jesus compelled the community to act for the sake of the world.

In Jerusalem and Antioch, large numbers of persons became followers of Jesus. These missional communities in two distinct contexts experienced the joy of welcoming new believers into the fellowship of Jesus followers.

As they devoted themselves to nurturing their relationship with the risen Savior, God formed a new community that proclaimed the lordship of Jesus Christ and embodied the gospel in ways that transformed the world. The church increased in number through the faithful living of these early Christians.

Ancient Pattern

Reflection on the congregations in Jerusalem and Antioch reveals three insights important for our purposes. First, the Holy Spirit formed a *new community*. Old distinctions based on religion or race crumbled when the gospel forged an assembly of God centered on the resurrected Lord.

Second, the new community *engaged in practices* that strengthened it as the body of Christ. God nurtured and shaped this new community as it studied the Scriptures and prayed together. Further, the new community engaged in practices that extended to others the grace it had received from God. They passionately proclaimed that Jesus had been crucified and buried, but that God raised Jesus from the dead. They expressed the love of God when they shared whatever they had with those in need and these acts of generosity had a formational impact on the church.

Third, their very existence gave *witness to God's mission* of redeeming the world and their practices showed them as participants in God's mission. This new community revealed God's ongoing story as it engaged in and invited others to step into God's story.

We believe the church today can benefit from following a similar pattern. We wrote this book to encourage the church in its spiritual practices as the body of Christ and its discernment of and participation in God's mission in the world.

Present Expressions of the Church

The church in North America, especially the evangelical expression of the church in which we have participated, has journeyed through a period that emphasized the experience of the individual believer. A review of the most frequently used songs in worship services or surveys of the most popular hymns reveal more "I" than "we." Some congregations have heralded their need-meeting ministries through which individuals and families can find help. Some pastors have preached sermon series that promise personal fulfillment more than spiritual maturity. Any one of these issues might not trouble us too much, but the pervasive nature of the individualization of Christianity creates grave concern.

We believe that Christians in North America need to rebuild their ecclesiology, and so we write with an emphasis on the corporate nature of the Christian faith. While individual response to the gospel is an essential element for a Christian, a congregation consists of more than the aggregate of individual believers. The corporate nature of the church is more than the sum of its parts. The Holy Spirit produced new communities in Jerusalem and Antioch and continues that work wherever two or three believers gather in Jesus' name.

One way to begin the revitalization of the church for those with a high view of the authority of Scripture could be as simple as recognizing that in much of the New Testament the writers addressed the church, not individuals. For example, when Paul wrote, "Let the same mind be in *you* that was in Christ Jesus" (Phil. 2:5, emphasis added), he used the plural pronoun that could be stated as *y'all*. Paul's admonition was not that an individual seek the mind of Christ, although he would not oppose that effort. Paul did not suggest that something good will come out of many individuals with the mind of Christ getting together, although that could have benefits. Paul urged the Philippian congregation, as a new community of the Spirit, to corporately live so that their common life looked like Jesus. The *ekklēsia* or "called out assembly" came into sharp focus when out of many individuals the Spirit created one body.

Ecclesial Practices

With the center of attention on the corporate body known as the church, our interest involves ecclesial practices. Much of the spiritual formation literature produced in the past several decades concentrated on the development of the person. We affirm the contribution of the spiritual formation movement that motivated many persons toward the goal of Christian maturity. To a large degree, however, the church has failed to apply a similar thoughtfulness to a more holistic Christian formation of the church. This book will add another voice to the consideration of the spiritual practices of the church.

We acknowledge the influence of John Wesley on our thinking in this regard, especially his sermon "The Means of Grace."[1] Wesley said, "By 'means of grace' I understand outward signs, words, or actions, ordained of God, and appointed for this end, to be the ordinary channels whereby [God] might convey to [humans] preventing [prevenient], justifying, or sanctifying grace." What Wesley called the means of grace observed "with the great congregation" we refer to as ecclesial practices. The means of grace involves those practices used by God to form God's people in Christlikeness.

People in the Wesleyan tradition classify some means of grace as *works of piety*. In the early church, the intentional study of the Scriptures and the apostles' teaching and the constant devotion to God through prayer were works of piety. Wesley added the celebration of the Lord's Supper as a third chief means of grace. Other practices with the primary goal of spiritual development include reflection on God's actions in small groups and worship with God's people.

Wesleyans classify other means of grace as *works of mercy*. When the congregations in Jerusalem and Antioch cared for the temporal needs of others, they engaged in the ecclesial practices of mercy. Other practices that offer God's grace to the world include compassionate service, hospitality, and generosity.

For both works of piety and works of mercy, Wesley insisted that "God is above all means" and that "there is no power" inherent in any ecclesial practice. Further, Wesley urged that people "seek God alone" as they engaged in the various means of grace and not to congratulate themselves "as having done some great thing."

Wesley's words of caution to those listening in the eighteenth century ring true today too. In no way do we suggest that the ecclesial practices we discuss in this book have a magical element that will bypass the work of the Holy Spirit. Instead, we believe that as we seek first the kingdom of God, the ecclesial practices will assist our endeavor.

God's Story

The missional church conversation begins with the conviction that God's mission involves the reconciliation of all creation to God's self. Some persons use the word "missional" without returning to God's mission as the starting place. To merely christen human-initiated endeavors as "missional" misses the point. We join those who insist that whatever Christians might do in ministry can best be understood as participation in what God has already initiated. This requires that the community of faith be involved in intentional listening and watching to discern God at work. Out of that discernment, then, the community can creatively explore ways to participate in God's mission.

A missional community will engage in ecclesial practices to be *shaped by God's story*. The community will reflect on what God has revealed about God's self. This is a theological task. The word "theology" literally refers to words (*logia*) about God (*theos*). In recent decades it seems that many persons in a congregation have been content to let the specialist (the preacher) do the work of a theologian, and many pastors have been willing to play that exclusive role. We believe that a pastor can best serve a congregation by facilitating the work of the entire congregation as it corporately gains an ever-increasing understanding of God. Through ecclesial practices such as the study of Scripture that reveals God's desire to redeem the whole world, prayer through which the congregation becomes sensitive to the movement of the Spirit, and discernment that traces the trajectory of God's mission throughout history, God forms the community as an effective participant in the *missio Dei* — God's mission. The missional community submits itself to the molding process of God's story by doing the work of theology, thinking about God.

A missional community will *proclaim God's story.* Just as the early church spoke of Jesus, so vibrant missional communities today tell of the resurrected Savior and Lord. We believe that in Jesus God does more than invite individuals into a personal relationship. The eternal reign of God has begun: "When [Jesus] had made purification for sins, he sat down at the right hand of the Majesty on high" (Heb. 1:3). As the church is aligned with God's mission and shaped by God's story, it boldly declares that the kingdom of God is at work in all of creation.

A missional community will *embody God's story.* When Jesus sent out the disciples, their actions to drive out demons and heal the sick served as a sign that "the kingdom of heaven has come near" (Matt. 10:7). The disciples who had been shaped by living with and learning from Jesus did more than just proclaim the good news. Their actions actually embodied the kingdom of God that they proclaimed. Yes, the kingdom of God will come in fullness at a future time, but the church lives today as an expression of the kingdom already begun. The missional community does more than talk about the reign of God; it actually embodies God's redemptive story in its life as the body of Christ.

The missional community seeks integrity between its actions and its intentions. In chapter 2 we consider maximizing that intent.

Exploration: Engagement in God's Story

❧ Describe what it is like to feel connected with a group of people. What contributes to the feeling of unity?

❧ As you consider the various practices mentioned in this chapter, which ones most resonate with you? Which seem natural practices in your missional community?

❧ Describe a time when you or your missional community provided a Christian witness without saying a word. What character qualities made that possible?

❧ Read Luke 11:5–10. How might your missional community more fully persevere in ecclesial practices?

❧ Pray for one another that your missional community will both proclaim and embody the grace of God.

Chapter 2

Signs of Grace

The Harmony and Rhythm of Life Together

WHEN BARNABAS FIRST VISITED THE CHRISTIANS IN ANTIOCH, he "saw the grace of God" (Acts 11:23). What does grace look like? What did Barnabas see that caused him to attribute it to God's grace?

Barnabas found in Antioch a diverse community that proclaimed Jesus as Lord. He witnessed the many people from various cultural contexts who became followers of Jesus. When Barnabas observed these actions of the congregation in Antioch, he understood them as God's grace at work. Barnabas saw the physical acts and understood them as a spiritual reality.

Semiotics is a study of the relationship between signs and the meaning to which the signs point. In contrast to linguistics, which examines the structure and meaning of language, semiotics looks at non-linguistic signs. In semiotics, the *iconic* — a sign that suggests a deeper meaning — directs attention to the *symbolic* — the meaning referenced in the sign.

Okay, we just jumped in the deep end. Where's the life ring? Let's try another story.

Luke wrote that Barnabas was a "good man" (Acts 11:24). What clues prompted Luke to come to that conclusion?

Earlier in the book of Acts, Luke described Barnabas as selling property and turning the money over to the apostles to distribute to those in need. This evidently is just one example of the way Barnabas conducted himself. Previously called Joseph, the apostles started calling him Barnabas, which means "son of encouragement," because of the way he conducted himself. When Luke reflected on Barnabas's generosity and cheerful spirit, Luke saw goodness, fullness of the Holy Spirit, and faith. All three of these qualities would not be visible on their own, but became discernible with some type of physical act.

In these examples of Barnabas and the missional communities in Antioch, what can be seen points to something beyond what can be seen. The *sign* points to the *signified*. Barnabas's generosity, a sign, demonstrated that he was a good man, the signified. The multicultural congregation in Antioch functioning as one body gave evidence of God's grace.

We make the connection between action and meaning all the time. When a young father gets up in the middle of the night to comfort an infant, the sleeping mother understands it as an act of love. When a teenager visits her widowed grandmother after school, the grandmother calls it a delight. When an employee arrives on time each day, the boss sees diligence. The physical action discloses a character quality.

Consider other accounts of the early church. Luke reported that following Pentecost the Christians in Jerusalem regularly had meals together, an act that Luke said signified "glad and generous hearts" (Acts 2:46). The believers shared everything, an act that signified they were of "one heart and soul" (Acts 4:32). This freedom in sharing and "their testimony to the resurrection of the Lord Jesus" showed that "great grace was upon them all" (Acts 4:33).

When Luke considered the fact that many persons came to believe in Jesus through the witness of the Christians in Antioch, he concluded that the "hand of the Lord was with them" (Acts 11:21). God is spirit and no one has seen the hand of the Lord except in a *sign* that pointed to the *signified*.

But sometimes the sign and the signified get out of sync. When a teenage boy forces himself on a teenage girl, he calls it love but she feels violated. When a salesperson waxes eloquent about the benefits of an overpriced item an elderly woman buys but cannot

Marks of the Missional Church

use, her family considers it deception. When a coach insists that the kids must function as a team but his son plays the whole game while others stand on the sideline, the players hear the speech as self-serving. In these instances, the physical sign failed to indicate the intended meaning.

The sign must be properly aligned with the signified. Charles Peirce,[1] in his discussion of semiotics, said that the iconic is *indexed* to the symbolic, that is, the sign *accurately* points to the signified.

Consider this contrast that shows an indexicalic dilemma. Barnabas sold a field and brought the proceeds to the apostles. Barnabas's action showed him as a "good man." For Barnabas, the sign is indexed with the signified. In contrast, Ananias and Sapphira sold property and pretended to give the proceeds to the apostles when in fact they kept some of the money for themselves. Their action did not accurately align with what they intended to depict. The physical action was out of sync with the intended meaning. They paid for their deception with their lives.

Church Signs

In *Changing Signs of Truth: A Christian Introduction to the Semiotics of Communication*, Crystal Downing affirms God's essential truths. Downing clearly receives from the Christian tradition an orthodox understanding of God and the church. Using the sophisticated constructs of semiotics for guidance, Downing urges the church to *(re)sign truth*[2] to best communicate the gospel in a changed and changing culture. Because of numerous influences, the church in many places has become misaligned with the gospel. What the church does is out of sync with what the church proclaims.

The United States flag has a prominent position in some sanctuaries; throughout the Gospels, Jesus called people of faith to put God above family and civil authority. Televangelists promise prosperity as God's blessing; Paul urged the church to follow Jesus' example and give itself away. Ushers remove a mother with her special-needs son from a worship service; Jesus welcomed children when the disciples tried to shoo them away.

A dire need today is for the church to examine whether what the church does closely aligns with what the church believes.

This issue intensifies in light of the profound cultural change we experience where the church's voice must be crystal clear. When the physical sign is out of sync with the signified, steps must be taken to restore the indexicality.

In an article for *The Huffington Post,* Tim Suttle lamented the sentimentality that has infected the church. Too many people attend a congregation as consumers, hoping to feel better about decisions they have already made. Instead of Jesus' teaching that "up is down, in is out, and nothing short of dying to ourselves and each other can help us truly live,"[3] the sentimental churchgoer wants to feel better. This motivation is out of whack with the Bible's description of a faithful disciple.

Leadership of a sentimental congregation, Tim continues, requires a pragmatism that provides exactly what the people want. Congregational leaders face immense pressure to increase market share until the bigger and better updraft carries them into the stratosphere. Unfortunately, these commitments ignore the cruciform life Jesus exemplified. "The church's job is not to grow—not even survive. The church's job is to die — continually — on behalf of the world, believing that with every death there is a resurrection."[4]

Tim's family and one other started heartland.k10 church in 2003. Driven by sentimentality and pragmatism, the congregation quickly grew to 200 families. But then they began to discern that their methods warred against the gospel. Their congregational practices and leadership priorities distorted God's story, which involves giving up power, laying down one's life, and sacrificial service for the sake of the world.[5]

The congregation changed its name to Redemption Church so that their identification would more closely align with their mission. They began to emphasize faithfulness in their participation in God's redemptive work. Now, they intentionally nurture an authentic, loving community as a place where spiritual seekers will be shaped by the teachings of Jesus. Every time they gather, they pray, "Lord, teach us how to love each other, and how to love the world around us for your sake."[6]

Marks of the Missional Church

Redemption Church deliberately aligns their ecclesial practices with God's story. They seek to live more purely so that they move in the flow of God's continuing work of redemption of the world. To do so, Redemption Church engages in God's story in such a way that the sign aligns with the signified, that the physical actions accurately point to God moving through God's people for the sake of the world.

The Rhythm of a Missional Community

In seeking to align the sign with the signified, missional communities will be intentional about developing ecclesial practices through which they participate in God's story. Over time the community develops a *rhythm* to its works of piety and works of mercy.

Some leaders in the Christian church in North America have applied lessons from the business world to congregational life. One such model is the SWOT analysis: strengths, weaknesses, opportunities, and threats. As leaders in an organization discuss these four areas, they seek to identify how strengths can maximize opportunities and minimize threats and how weaknesses can be overcome so as not to hinder opportunities nor nourish threats. Out of this type of exercise a mission statement may emerge with goals for the group and objectives for various initiatives.

Nothing intrinsic in this type of process, however, will cause a group to fully engage in God's story so that they are shaped by and actually embody God's story. The steps in such an agenda may not detract from the congregation's mission, but it does not require that the community be immersed in God's story.

Instead of doing something in the hope that somehow the activity will be beneficial (that is, doing something to accomplish a set goal), we suggest that a missional community actually involve itself in practices known to further God's purposes in this world. Rather than setting goals, we propose that the missional community agree on a rhythm of life. Through the rhythm of its shared life with intentional ecclesial practices, the missional community will begin to take on the complexion and character of the Christ they proclaim.

In church history we find times when Christian communities established a rule of life. Contrary to what some people might envision when they hear this term, this is not a set of rules or a checklist to maintain. It is not some standard that exists outside of the community as some type of objective measure.

By rule of life we mean a pattern of shared life. Sometimes the pattern emerged in an organic, spontaneous manner such as what is seen in Jerusalem after Pentecost. In other places in the Bible we hear an invitation to intentional rhythms. Peter, for example, urged his readers to "make every effort to support your faith with goodness, and goodness with knowledge, and knowledge with self-control, and self-control with endurance, and endurance with godliness, and godliness with mutual affection, and mutual affection with love" (2 Pet. 1:5–7). In a similar manner, Paul advised the Ephesians to "lead a life worthy of the calling to which you have been called, with all humility and gentleness, with patience, bearing with one another in love, making every effort to maintain the unity of the Spirit in the bond of peace" (Eph. 4:1–3). Both Peter and Paul encouraged Christians to establish a pattern of living out the faith.

We hope you will become more aware of the organic rhythms that arise from your particular context. We encourage your missional community to pay attention to how God works within and through it and to make adjustments as needed to better align with God's mission. In addition to the spontaneous rhythm that develops, we urge you to make corporate decisions that seek to nurture the spiritual life of the community. Decide as a community on those ecclesial practices through which you "may become participants of the divine nature" (2 Pet. 1:4).

At the end of the chapters we provide suggestions for conversation in your missional community. We recommend that you eventually write down the values of your community and the practices in which you will engage as an expression of those values. When you put your corporate rule of life in writing, use a form that makes sense to the community. Draft your statements on ecclesial practices in simple and manageable terms.

We have one more topic to cover in this introduction. In chapter 3 we look at the four marks of the church from the Nicene Creed that we used to structure the book.

Exploration: The Harmony and Rhythm of Life Together

❧ Think of someone you consider a "good" person. What actions (signs) indicate the goodness (signified)?

❧ Consider your missional community and compassionate service or another work of mercy. What particular actions (signs) point to God's love (signified)?

❧ Read Ephesians 4:1–3. What practices might help your missional community "lead a life worthy of the calling to which you have been called"?

❧ Throughout this book we will consider elements that could become part of a corporate rule of life. What elements are already parts of the fabric of your missional community? Especially consider elements that may have been assumed but not articulated. What elements would you like to be part of your life together as the body of Christ?

❧ Describe the weekly pattern of your missional community or a weekly pattern you envision for your group. Does this rhythm facilitate full engagement in God's mission? What adjustments might improve your missional community's participation in the *missio Dei*?

❧ Pray with each other, asking God to help you discern God's will for your missional community.

Chapter 3

Credo

We Believe

PAUL REMINDED THE CONGREGATION IN CORINTH OF THE GOSPEL he proclaimed to them: "that Christ died . . . was buried . . . was raised on the third day" (1 Cor. 15:3–4). In a concise manner, Paul stated the basics of the Christian faith. Paul used a similar approach in his letter to the congregation in Colossae: Jesus is "the image of the invisible God, the firstborn of all creation . . . all things have been created through him and for him . . . He is the head of the body, the church" (Col. 1:15–16, 18). In this passage Paul outlined key elements of our understanding of the person and role of Jesus in creation and reconciliation.

A creed does the same thing. Derived from the Latin word *credo*, which means "I believe," a creed states a formal summary of what Christians believe in a succinct way. Leaders at various times in church history created a creed to articulate the articles of faith.

Christians today continue to use two ancient creeds in worship. The Apostles' Creed is traditionally used in baptisms since this creed follows a Trinitarian pattern, as does the baptismal ritual. Through the creed, the person says, "I believe in God, the Father almighty . . . in Jesus Christ . . . in the Holy Spirit." In baptism, the presiding minister says, "I baptize you in the name of the Father, and of the Son, and of the Holy Spirit."

The Nicene Creed is longer and has more theological detail than the Apostles' Creed. The Nicene Creed first developed in 325 during a time of great debate on the deity of Christ. Bishops adopted the Nicene Creed as a way to state concisely the orthodox understanding of Jesus as both human and divine.

An expanded form of the Nicene Creed emerged in 381. This version included what people have called the four marks of the church: one, holy, catholic, apostolic. A *mark* refers to a sign used to identify the nature of the church that is common in all times and places.

But as discussed in the previous chapter, the actual behavior of the church could contradict the descriptive marks. In that case, utilizing the terminology of semiotics, the relationship between the iconic action and the symbolic meaning is not properly indexed when the church's action does not align with the church's nature.

Some have accounted for such a misalignment by suggesting that the *invisible* church was ideal and perfect while the *visible* church was less than ideal and imperfect. When people looked at the church and found ungodliness, for example, they explained the discrepancy by pointing to the purity of the spiritual realm. While there may be discord in the visible church, some might say, unity exists in the invisible church.

Others took a proactive approach to the disparity. When they looked at the four marks of the church, they found the implication of both gifts and tasks. For example, since God has made the church one, a gift of grace, the church should strive toward unity, a task. Since God has made the church holy, the church should strive toward perfect love.

Charles Van Engen took this notion a step further when he suggested reflecting on the four marks of the church as adverbs as well as adjectives. In its traditional form, the four adjectives modify the noun *church*. Van Engen proposed that the four marks move from merely descriptors of the church to consideration as accompanying actions as well. For Van Engen, the "one Church of Jesus Christ would be seen as a unifying force . . . the holy Church of Jesus would be seen as a sanctifying force . . . the catholic Church of Jesus Christ would be seen as a reconciling force . . . the apostolic

Marks of the Missional Church

Church of Jesus Christ would be seen as a proclaiming force."[1] The marks of the church, then, not only describe the nature of the church, but also set the rhythm of activities in which the church engages.

We use this active sense of the four marks throughout the book. The ecclesial practices we discuss form ways a missional community can exemplify the marks. When the church embodies in concrete acts what it believes, as empowered by the Holy Spirit, the church becomes in real time what it is by God's design.

We follow the lead of Darrell Guder and George Hunsberger and present the four marks of the church in reverse order.[2] Guder and Hunsberger, part of The Gospel and Our Culture Network, suggested that flipping the order restores mission to the theological understanding of the church. The order of the four marks, they say, influences understanding. For example, beginning with the characteristic "one" tends to create an inward perspective of the church. By the time a person gets to the fourth mark, then, the term "apostolic" tends to be understood in terms of apostolic succession. This creates a backward tilt when the concept of apostolic has a forward trajectory. Beginning with "apostolic," on the other hand, immediately sets the perspective looking out on the reconciling work of God still in process. The emphasis becomes seeking to emulate how the apostles lived in order to continue apostolic mission.

Guiding Sentence

Apostolic. Catholic. Holy. One. Too often with lists like this, people tend to build silos for each element even though the elements interact with and influence each other. So we conceive of the marks of the missional church in this holistic way:

> The church participates in God's mission by proclaiming
> to the whole world — all classes and cultures, all ages
> and genders, all nationalities and races — that God is
> holy love and, through Jesus, God is transforming a

people who embody that holy love as empowered and knit together by the Holy Spirit, a sign that the kingdom of God is here.

We will unpack this statement mark by mark in the opening chapter of parts II, III, IV, and V.

Missional Church

Emil Brunner wrote that "the church exists by mission as fire exists by burning."[3] No mission, no church. In *Marks of the Missional Church* we seek to expand an understanding of the church by exploring ecclesial practices of the missional church. Our hope is that the *signs* visible in the ecclesial practices enhance the awareness of and appreciation for the church as Christ's body, the *signified*.

In the fourth century, during the time in which bishops crafted the Nicene Creed, a partnership between the church, the empire, and the wider culture began. In the preceding centuries the church faced stiff persecution. That changed when Constantine issued the Edict of Milan in 313 that directed governmental leaders to accept Christians and offer restitution when needed. Now under the protection of the state, the church changed dramatically. The privileged position of the church allowed some things formerly in the shadows to step into the light, but at times led to corruption and misuse of power.

Evidence suggests that the relationship between church and society has entered another time of transition. In what some call post-Christendom, the church no longer holds an advantaged position in society in many places. Some Christians lament this development. Others — and we count ourselves in this group — believe that the disruptive change we are experiencing provides an opportunity for the re-formation of the church.

To find a way forward during what sometimes seems like chaos, the church must return to its theological core. In this book we explore ecclesiology, what we believe about God's intent for the church. More specifically, we look at how the nature of the church works itself out in concrete ways. How does the church articulate the gospel? How might the church embody the gospel? We now begin to reflect on those questions.

Exploration: We Believe

᠙ Read together the Nicene Creed.

᠙ What statements seem clear to you? What statements seem difficult to understand?

᠙ Van Egan suggested that the four marks of the church in the Nicene Creed be considered as adverbs as well as adjectives. Describe how the apostolic church might act as a proclaiming force. Describe how the church catholic might act as a reconciling force. Describe how the holy church might act as a sanctifying force. Describe how the one church might act as a unifying force.

᠙ Say the following together: *the church participates in God's mission by proclaiming to the whole world — all classes and cultures, all ages and genders, all nationalities and races — that God is holy love and, through Jesus, God is transforming a people who embody that holy love as empowered and knit together by the Holy Spirit, a sign that the kingdom of God is here.* What word or phrase lingers in your thinking a bit longer than the rest?

᠙ Pray for one another that your missional community will embody the apostolic, catholic, holy, and one nature of the church.

Part II

Apostolic

The church participates in God's mission by proclaiming to the whole world — all classes and cultures, all ages and genders, all nationalities and races — that God is holy love and, through Jesus, God is transforming a people who embody that holy love as empowered and knit together by the Holy Spirit, a sign that the kingdom of God is here.

Ecclesial Practices

Discerning God's Mission Together

Praying Together

Witnessing of God's Grace Together

2 Corinthians 5:14–21

For the love of Christ urges us on, because we are convinced that one has died for all; therefore all have died. And he died for all, so that those who live might live no longer for themselves, but for him who died and was raised for them. From now on, therefore, we regard no one from a human point of view; even though we once knew Christ from a human point of view, we know him no longer in that way. So if anyone is in Christ, there is a new creation: everything old has passed away; see, everything has become new! All this is from God, who reconciled us to himself through Christ, and has given us the ministry of reconciliation; that is, in Christ God was reconciling the world to himself, not counting their trespasses against them, and entrusting the message of reconciliation to us. So we are ambassadors for Christ, since God is making his appeal through us; we entreat you on behalf of Christ, be reconciled to God. For our sake he made him to be sin who knew no sin, so that in him we might become the righteousness of God.

Chapter 4

Apostolic Church

2 Corinthians 5:14–21

C OMPOSING SOME LETTERS DOES NOT COME EASILY. THE LETTERS exchanged between the apostle Paul and the Corinthian congregation certainly posed a challenge. The apostle Paul and the Corinthians had a thorny relationship that persisted. Hurt and confusion led to the exchange of frank and impassioned words.

Biblical scholars have detected evidence of as many as five letters between the missionary and the congregation he planted in Corinth, but only two remain. In the period between the first and second letters Paul experienced a humiliating visit to Corinth. But Paul kept reaching out. By the time the progression of events comes to chapter 5 of the fourth letter (which in the Bible is 2 Corinthians), Paul had laid the theological groundwork to launch a soaring reflection on reconciliation. This passage reaches the heights of the gospel for a very earthly challenge.

Paul declared that messengers of the gospel do not proclaim themselves, yet their lives are inseparable from their message. "You yourselves are our letter, written on our hearts, to be known and read by all; and you show that you are a letter of Christ . . . written not with ink but with the Spirit of the living God, not on tablets of stone but on tablets of human hearts" (2 Cor. 3:2–3).

The apostle understood well that reconciliation sits at the epicenter of all that God aims for in the world. Reconciliation became the posture by which Paul approached the congregation that had caused him pain. He reminded them that because of their transformation as those made righteous by the death and resurrection of Jesus, the whole world will read their story and know about God's salvation. He challenged the Corinthians to put on their God lenses. He sought restored relationship for the sake of the good news of the gospel. The veracity of their proclamation concerning God's reconciliation depended on their restored relationship.

Paul did not work in a vacuum when he wrote about the compelling love of Christ urging the church onward, or the transformed life in Christ, or the ministry of reconciliation. He wrote with specific people in mind. Paul's authority as an apostle was questioned, but God's reconciling purposes took precedence to those personal concerns. Paul's words on reconciliation clearly showed the already/not-yet tension of living within God's reign of love.

Even today, Christians continually live with this tension. God's initiative of reconciliation is realized in the lives of believers, but it will continue until the completion of time.

So Paul wrote difficult letters. He wrote out of pain and sadness, but motivated by the desperate hope for the Corinthians to receive the full-orbed gospel of reconciliation on a cosmic scale. Paul knew that the conflict he faced was not the totality of the story. Christ died for *everyone*. Christ sides with *all* people. Christ is resurrected and the power of reconciliation is unleashed in that life. New creation is creeping in, replacing the old, transforming the planet. God's mission rests on reconciliation so that all people may be included in God's grand-scale love story. And we are the ambassadors of this good news (2 Cor. 5:20).

Collect

> *God of unconditional love,*
> *Who relentlessly offers life to all;*
> *Do not count our brokenness against us, but make us*
> *   a new creation*

So that we may effectively serve as ambassadors of
   your reconciling mission;
Bathed in divine love, we praise your name.
Amen.

An Open Letter to the World

God's church is first and foremost sent. The word *apostle*, meaning "sent," reveals that the apostolic church consists of an active community on a mission initiated by God, commissioned by Christ, and empowered by the Holy Spirit. The early church came to life because of the impassioned work of the apostles. Convinced that they had received the gospel in fullness, they became pioneers of living in the way of Christ. The first apostles did not keep the message of God's salvation to themselves. Instead, they emulated Jesus who invited them to *follow* him, *go* and make disciples, and *tell* the good news.

God's church is sent because God is a sending God. From the beginning of God's story recorded in Scripture, we see God intersecting with the lives of God's people by sending forth God's word in creation, by sending holy messengers, by sending God's people to new lands toward new promises, by sending God's people as a light to the nations.

The triune God has always been on the move: creating, relating, transforming, and reconciling. Not surprising, then, after his resurrection Jesus commissioned his disciples to "go and make disciples of all nations" (Matt. 28:19). Jesus' next set of instructions was to not leave Jerusalem until "the Father sends you the gift he promised" (Acts 1:4 NLT). On the day of Pentecost the believers received that gift: the Holy Spirit. They were empowered to leave the upper room as witnesses to God's love. God's church is apostolic, then, sent on God's mission, because it is God's nature to give love away.

The church forms God's open letter to the world. *Read this!* God says to the world. *Through this letter written not with pen and ink but with my living Spirit, you will understand who I am. Come and read and understand redemption's story.*

Understanding the apostolic nature of church requires considering what it means to be a sent people. In 2 Corinthians 5 we learn about three pulses in the rhythm of the witnessing church: the apostolic church is *compelled, reconciled,* and *commissioned as ambassador.*

God's love *compels* the apostolic church to proclaim the good news. The divine love story reveals God as the initiator of salvation. We humbly receive God's gift. Even though human ability to choose independence over interdependence has broken fellowship with God, God desires reconciliation with the whole creation. Such an incredible gift prompts the church to tell God's story. Love generates love. We-who-are-loved are sent to love others. Christ's love urges us on. We read God's letter to us and are compelled to read it aloud to the world. The story cannot be kept secret.

Christ lived a life emptied of everything but love and so provides an example of this compulsion. When Jesus faced death on a cross as a condemned criminal, God's love motivated his obedience. The spiritual authorities of the day could not accept such extravagant love and worked to silence the scandalous love letter. But they could not hush the bold declarations. The church lives as the postscript to God's open letter to the world through Christ's love.

God's love is a non-coercive, freeing grace at work in the lives of those who choose to cooperate. God has granted the liberty to say *no.* This is the delicacy of love: love is fullest and richest when it is freest.

God's transforming power prompts the apostolic church to declare the good news of *reconciliation.* The defining act of God is reconciliation and love is the defining force. Paul claimed that "if anyone is in Christ, there is a new creation: everything old has passed away; see everything has become new" (2 Cor. 5:17). This passage hinges on two phrases: *if anyone* and *in Christ.* The initiative and the good work of salvation are God's in Christ. Humans do not generate salvation. The doors of reconciliation are open to anyone only if they choose to participate. The sent church continually issues the invitation to live in Christ.

Finally, God's gracious invitation prompts the apostolic church to eagerly serve as God's *ambassadors in Christ*. An ambassador speaks on behalf of another as an advocate, representative, or messenger. When the church gives creedal affirmation to being apostolic, it affirms the active role Christ's body takes as the collective witness to God's salvation. God's church is the communal ambassador of God's story.

Paul said, "God is making his appeal through us" (2 Cor. 5:20). God's call to the church does not get any clearer than that. Jesus claimed that, after his ascension, his sent ones would do far greater things than he had done. How is it possible for humans to do greater things than the Son of God? This is the paradox of the apostolic church: a community of frail humans has become the living, breathing body of Christ.

The church is God's open letter to the world, telling the story of the reign of love on earth. Two billion Christians today can tell a deep and broad account of God's story, something a solitary prophet could not do. The waiting and hurting world depends on the church to read God's open letter and understand the message of reconciliation.

Apostolicity in Motion

The apostolic church must discern God's mission as it goes where God sends (see chapter 5). Discerning God's mission requires eyes to see and ears to hear. God's apostolic church must be steeped in the Scriptures and traditions of the church to understand the trajectory of God's story through the ages. Not content to wait for seekers to find them, the sent ones go to where people need the good news. When the apostolic church finds people who need God's favor, the ambassadors respond out of love for God.

The apostolic church lives in the rhythm of prayer (see chapter 6). Prayer is the practice of waking up to the presence of God. Prayer is the practice of posturing to hear and be heard. Prayer is the practice of communicating honestly and passionately with God. Prayer changes the way we live and move and have our being. Prayer activates even a mustard seed faith. Prayer aligns us with the heart and will of God. When the apostolic church prays, it makes an intentional turn toward God to be formed into the image of God.

The apostolic church witnesses to God's grace (see chapter 7). In doing so, the church serves as an ambassador of God's reconciliation. Witnesses tell what they have seen, what they have heard, and how they have been transformed. Because the church forms the first fruits of the new creation, the church must tell all who will listen about the beautiful gift of this new life. To know God's grace is to speak of God's grace.

Mission: Possible

Our mission, should we choose to accept it, is to live reconciled with God and each other. This would be an impossible mission without the transformative and empowering love of God to fuel our lives as ambassadors.

Paul wrote painful letters and persevered through a humiliating relationship with the Corinthians in confidence that reconciliation would win the day. Compelled by God's love letter written to the world in the life of Christ, Paul would not stop until reconciliation had reached every corner of creation.

> *The church participates in God's mission by proclaiming to the whole world — all classes and cultures, all ages and genders, all nationalities and races — that God is holy love and, through Jesus, God is transforming a people who embody that holy love as empowered and knit together by the Holy Spirit, a sign that the kingdom of God is here.*

Marked as apostolic, God's *church participates in God's mission by proclaiming to the whole world* the good news. God makes the appeal of reconciliation through us, the church in the twenty-first century. Let us become apostles of this mission so that the world might clearly read and know God's open letter of love.

Benediction

May the loving, creative, reconciling God assure you of God's blessing, grace, and love so that the world will see in you God's open letter of reconciliation. Amen.

Exploration: Apostolic Church

❧ Pray the collect together.

❧ Describe a time when you worked to restore a relationship with someone, maybe by writing a letter or email. What emotions did you feel in that process? What was the result?

❧ Read 2 Corinthians 5:18–19 and 21. Describe how you understand the church as God's open letter to the world. Why do you suppose God entrusted the message of reconciliation to us?

❧ What is the role of an apostle? Why would those who crafted the Nicene Creed consider apostolicity as one of the four most important characteristics of the church?

❧ Describe the ways in which you see your missional community as sent by God. Where might God be sending your missional community as participants in God's mission of reconciliation?

❧ Speak the benediction as a blessing to one another and as a call to action in God's mission.

Chapter 5

Perceptive Listening

Discerning God's Mission Together

T HAT WOULD BE WONDERFUL, BUT GOOD LUCK DOING IT HERE."
"Sounds like a great idea although I'm not sure it will last."
"I'd be in favor, but will it work in a place like this?"

These were the kinds of responses voiced as members of The Open Door and Valley View Church went door to door in the Garfield neighborhood of Pittsburgh, Pennsylvania. They walked the streets to gauge residents' interest in reclaiming an unused and neglected plot of land for the purpose of starting an urban community farm.

Months before, leaders from The Open Door had met to consider how best to incarnate the gospel in the place to which they had been called. They asked tough questions. They debated. They prayed. The Open Door had started a few years earlier in another part of the city, but had recently found a permanent home in the Garfield area. They eagerly wanted their missional community to more fully reflect the racial and economic diversity of the neighborhood around them. Initial ideas focused on how to make their gatherings more attractive to residents. But as they prayed and sought God's guidance, it became clear that the Spirit was leading them to focus on ministry outside the walls of the church building.

About that time, pastors John and BJ attended a conference in which they learned about another missional community that

49

was doing ecological restoration and sustainable agriculture. They were inspired and intrigued. John and BJ gathered people from The Open Door and Valley View Church, a historic congregation in the Garfield neighborhood. Together, these missional communities began to dream about how God could use them to make an urban farm a reality. In an area of Pittsburgh pockmarked by abandoned and neglected properties, God led them to a plot of land just three blocks from Valley View's building. One year later, Garfield Community Farm came into existence.

Today the farm thrives and has added a second location with the clear vision to bless the citizens of Garfield. John leads a dynamic team of neighborhood volunteers. Many area organizations partner together to tend to the farm's growth. Diverse crops are produced each year, all of which are made available to residents of the neighborhood. The farm provides for families experiencing food scarcity through discounted shares and work-sharing options. Volunteers also provide environmental and holistic health education on-site.

The decision to start Garfield Community Farm was not the first thing that came to mind when The Open Door community initially asked how they could reach out to their city. Through the practice of active discernment, however, God led this missional community to a creative ministry that has helped The Open Door respond to the needs of their neighborhood in transformative ways.

Collect

> *Ever-creating God,*
> *Who is constantly bringing about new life in the*
> *world;*
> *Open our ears*
> *So that we may discern your voice, have our minds*
> *renewed, and know your will;*
> *For the sake of your glory.*
> *Amen.*

Ongoing Creation

"We believe in one God, the Father, the Almighty, maker of heaven and earth, of all that is, seen and unseen." The opening line of the Nicene Creed confesses that God is the creator of the cosmos. God's creative activity did not end once the world was made. Orthodox Christian theology rejects any notion of a god who set the world in motion and then stepped back to watch it spin, uninvolved and distant. The One who spoke the universe into existence still speaks. The Maker's work continues, moment by moment.

The same is true of God's redeeming work. While the death of Christ was "once for all" (Heb. 7:27), the benefits of his sacrificial death and resurrection are an ongoing reality in the world. When the gospel is heard and people, awakened by the Spirit, respond in faith, "there is a new creation: everything old has passed away; see, everything has become new!" (2 Cor. 5:17).

The ever-creating and redeeming God beckons God's image-bearing people to join in the ongoing work of restoring and renewing creation. Just as Adam and Eve were charged to steward the earth (Gen. 1:28), Christ has given the church the "ministry of reconciliation" (2 Cor. 5:18b). God's people are invited to participate in the reconciling work of Christ in the world.

Christ does not give us a mission and leave us to accomplish it alone. The Holy Spirit guides and empowers the church. After commissioning his disciples, Jesus promised, "I am with you always, to the end of the age" (Matt. 28:20). Since Christ is the Good Shepherd (John 10:11), connection to him and attentiveness to his voice are essential to faithful engagement in God's mission.

The need for discernment becomes especially clear when we try to do ministry apart from it. The Gospel of Mark records how Jesus' disciples tried unsuccessfully to drive out a malevolent spirit from a young boy. As a result, the disciples were pulled into a fruitless argument with the scribes (Mark 9:14). After Jesus arrived and finally drove out the spirit and healed the boy, the disciples asked why they could not. He replied, "This kind can come out only through prayer" (Mark 9:29).

The practice of discerning God's mission brings direction and focus to the life of the church. It can help a dying or stalled community truly shift to reaching out in risk-taking ways. Discernment helps move us from mere good intentions to concrete investment in the kingdom, from talk to action. Through discernment we attempt to gain knowledge and wisdom so that we may detect not only what God is calling us to do but also how we might best go about doing this.

Discernment involves heeding the promptings of the Holy Spirit and listening to the needs of the world around us. It comes through attentiveness to God's voice through prayer, Scripture, the Christian tradition, and community discussion and learning. When God's people enter into the process of discernment, we are asking God to speak to us and instill in us a holy imagination. As we listen and sense God's direction, the ways we can creatively and meaningfully enter into the work of redemption become clear. Sometimes they are discovered in an instant. Often discernment comes over a period of days, weeks, or years to those who wait patiently before the Lord.

Mission does not originate with us nor is it something humans can dictate or control. In fact, when we fail to prayerfully discern God's voice we can actually short-circuit what God desires to do through us. Mission begins in the heart of our Creator God and flows through God's people to the world. For the church to speak the gospel powerfully, we must first learn to listen carefully.

Quiet Reflection

The four Gospels reveal that Jesus often withdrew to a quiet place. No doubt the stresses of ministry and the pressing crowds necessitated this. Jesus did this for a specific reason: to pray. During these times of retreat, our Lord realigned his vision and direction for ministry. He bared his soul in prayer and listened attentively to his Father's voice. Out of these experiences of God's presence, Jesus then poured out his life in intentional, active service to others.

The practice of retreat is an invaluable tool to missional communities that seek to discern God's direction in ministry. While many spiritual life retreats center on the development of the interior life of the individual, a retreat that focuses on the community's outward vision can create intentional space for the whole community to discern God's will for the future. Focused times of prayer, teaching, searching the Scriptures, and honest discussion can bring clarity and excitement to the community's next steps.

When engaging the missional community in the process of discernment, some might be tempted to listen only to the voices of the articulate, resourced, and experienced. A better way will include women and men from various generations, life experiences, and stages of spiritual maturity. This can often create a healthy dissonance and raise necessary questions that lend critical insights into God's mission for a particular place and time.

Discernment also includes being awakened to the needs of the world around us. One church feared becoming inward focused. They wanted to engage in risk-taking ministry but were not sure what to do next. One Sunday morning, the leadership surprised the congregation after the opening prayer in worship. Instead of continuing on with a normal service, all of the worshipers were loaded onto buses and driven through the church's neighborhood, including a stop right in front of a local drug house.

That experience inspired a large group of men from the church to set up a neighborhood barbecue and camp out right outside the doors of the house, effectively closing down the illicit business. This effort multiplied until the church had mobilized the neighborhood to close down several drug houses. Awareness led to creative, Spirit-inspired action.

Research can also aid a community in the process of discernment. This may not sound like a spiritual discipline at first, but the formal gathering and analysis of data for the purpose of mission is actually a practice of biblical wisdom. The writer of the Proverbs affirms that "without counsel, plans go wrong, but with many advisers they succeed" (Prov. 15:22).

People of one congregation had a growing discomfort with their lack of attention to the needs of their neighbors. They came to the conclusion that they possessed the desire to help, but lacked concrete information on how to do so. Without this critical data they could have moved forward, but may have ended up trying to address needs that did not really exist.

Instead, the congregation developed a simple five-question survey that guided their conversations with area residents. Not only did this effort increase the connection between the congregation and their neighbors, it also yielded helpful and surprising information. Because of this survey the congregation identified several acute needs they felt they could address. In this case the entire community, whether part of the congregation or not, became active participants in this missional community's process of discernment.

Persistent Attention

The Open Door had a simple desire to join God's mission for the sake of the neighborhood in which they lived. This desire led them on a process of learning and discovery out of which the Garfield Community Farm began. Though the vision was large and the barriers were numerous, they remained confident of God's direction. On what used to be abandoned and neglected lots, two vibrant urban farms now stand that have become sources of both physical and spiritual nourishment for the East End of Pittsburgh.

Discernment takes sustained focus to heed the voice of the Spirit and identify God's desired response to the needs that exist in our cities and neighborhoods. When a missional community commits to discern God's mission together, it leads to exciting opportunities as the hands and feet of Christ in the world.

Benediction

May the eternal God, in whom the future presently resides, draw you into the will of God as you listen intently for the voice of God and to the cries of your

neighbors while you confidently go wherever Love leads.
Amen.

Exploration: Discerning God's Mission Together

❧ Pray the collect together.

❧ What emotions do you think The Open Door members experienced as they walked door to door asking neighbors in the Garfield community about the possibility of a community farm?

❧ Describe a time when doubters questioned the prudence of something your missional community believed that God directed you to do.

❧ Prayer can easily be reduced to asking God for things we want or need. How is discerning prayer different from intercessory prayer?

❧ Read Psalm 119:105. Read, quote, or paraphrase a Bible verse that provides direction to your missional community.

❧ How are decisions made in your missional community? What adjustments to the process might better facilitate discernment of God's direction? How might a more diverse group of people become involved in the discernment process?

❧ Read James 1:5. How can you include times of corporate prayer for discernment in the rhythms of your missional community?

❧ Speak the benediction as a blessing to one another and as a call to action in God's mission.

Chapter 6

Awakening to God

Praying Together

WHEN RENE ENTERED THE CARE HOUSE IN SEARCH OF FOOD, she was too dispirited to make eye contact with the volunteers who served her. She feared that her burden of shame might crush her into dust.

The Care House exists to feed both body and soul through "food, prayer, and friendship." A food pantry of sorts, the Care House seeks to alleviate hunger and suffering of persons living in the neighborhood.

The manager of the Care House, Monica, stood at the door to welcome guests as she did every weekday at the one o'clock opening. Prompted to connect with the burdened guest, Monica gently placed a hand on Rene's shoulder. "Are you doing okay today?" Monica asked. The mumbled response caused her to prod, "Do you need to talk?" The women went into a prayer room at the front of the house.

"I'm a forty-eight year old woman," Rene said. "I shouldn't be living like this, strung out on meth."

Monica heard the confession and silently asked God to touch Rene. Monica gently introduced Rene to the God who welcomes all persons no matter how lost they may feel. The women prayed together. Monica invited Rene to come to a brand new neighborhood fellowship and Scripture study called The Living Room.

As Rene left with food for the week, her parting words pierced Monica's heart. "You looked me in the eyes," Rene said. "No one ever does that." Monica watched Rene walk away from The Care House as her prayers for Rene continued.

Nampa Church is across the street from The Care House. On Saturday evenings the congregation's gymnasium is transformed into a Holy of Holies as people gather for a prayerful capstone to the week. Practicing a liturgy of thanksgiving and request, yielding and rejoicing, God's people gather to listen to and be heard through the ministry of prayer. In an effort to surrender the week's experiences and to prepare for the celebration of the *little resurrection* on Sunday morning, evening prayer forms a communal act of devotion. Members gather to place themselves in a posture of surrender. Stations throughout the room provide tactile ways to interact with God in prayer. Scriptural call and response anchors the prayer meeting.

Moved to create space to explore the spiritual discipline of prayer, Pastor James asked the community a simple question: *What if we created space to consecrate ourselves for holy lives of worship?* Evening prayer emerged out of the responses to that question.

Prayer changes the people of God. Prayer brings God's people into alignment with the heart of God whose mission is reconciliation.

Nampa Church is a long-established congregation with deep roots in the neighborhood. The congregation's stated mission is "A ministry of hope . . . at home, across the street, and around the world." Corporate and individual prayer guides and empowers that mission. On Wednesdays, willing participants fast from lunch and meet in the sanctuary for an hour of prayer. Various groups meet throughout the week to pray. God directs the mission of this congregation as they pray together.

Collect

> *God of the creative Word,*
> *Who constantly communicates with us through*
> *Scripture and stories, sunrise and stars;*

Tune our hearts to your voice
So that we may have ears to hear and hearts to obey;
To the glory of the One who walks with us.
Amen.

God Who Speaks

Christ, the eternal Word, already existed in the beginning. This is what the pastor-poet-prophet John tells us in the prologue to his gospel-witness to Jesus' life, death, and resurrection (John 1:1–14). All that exists was created through the Word, the logos—the embodiment of wisdom. The Word gave life to everything that was created and brought light to everyone. This same light shines in the darkness, and the darkness can never extinguish it.

God's creative presence dwells with us and directly communicates with us through the life and light of our Savior, Jesus. The Word, John told us, became human and made his home among us. "He was full of unfailing love and faithfulness. And we have seen his glory" (John 1:14 NLT). We have been invited into relationship with a God who speaks, a God who wants us to hear directly from the source.

Examples of prayer in Scripture range from questions posed to God to the songs of praise and the mourning of poets to the angered complaints of depressed prophets to the agonizing pleas of Jesus the night before his murder to the collective searching prayers of the early church for guidance. Prayer is splashed across the stories of Scripture from start to finish and covers the gamut of human experience: from pleasure to panic to gratitude to complaint to grief to ecstasy to wonder to doubt to belief.

Basic communication theory states that messages are delivered through some medium, for example, language (verbal) or body language (non-verbal). All living creatures communicate through a complex exchange that involves the senses.

The relationship between humans and God is mediated through some form of communication. How we relate to God is determined by how both parties communicate. Our words, actions, and postures all influence this communication. The reverse is also true; the way God communicates through revelation in creation, Scripture, and human stories matters greatly. There are no unmediated interactions, including the God-human relationship.

The Psalms record many times when God's people cried for help and God heard their cries and saved them. These prayers were honest appeals for God to listen and save. Many times the Psalms affirm that God hears and responds. "Hear my cry, O God; listen to my prayer. From the end of the earth I call to you, when my heart is faint" (Ps. 61:1–2a). "Trust in him at all times, O people; pour out your heart before him; God is a refuge for us. . . . Once God has spoken; twice have I heard this: that power belongs to God, and steadfast love belongs to you, O Lord" (Ps. 62:8, 11–12a).

Prayer forms an essential element in our relationship with God. The way we relate to God in prayer changes the way we live. Prayer aligns us with God's heartbeat. When God's people pray God sharpens the *imago Dei*, God's image, in the church. Prayer magnifies God's loving presence in the world because prayer transforms us. Prayer shapes who we are and impacts how God is known on earth.

Prayer and prayers are not the same things. Barbara Brown Taylor, preacher and author, said that prayer is more than saying prayers at set times in the right places with the right words. "Prayer is waking up to the presence of God."[1]

When practicing the rhythm of prayer, God's apostolic church is reconciled to God, each other, and creation. Prayer is the practice of posturing ourselves to hear and be heard. Prayer is like a missional tune-up that brings God's people into alignment with God's aims and action for reconciliation.

Prayer as Habit

When Rene left The Care House after their first encounter, Monica was not sure she would see Rene again. But Monica did have her telephone number. So she called the following week to invite Rene to The Living Room, a ministry Monica started to be a place of belonging for guests of The Care House. No response. She tried again the following week. Since Rene did not answer, Monica left a message with another invitation. That Wednesday evening Monica spied Rene headed down the street and her heart fluttered with hope. Rene was actually the first person to attend The Living Room fellowship. She has hardly missed a gathering of The Living Room since that night. Together, they listen to Scripture, listen to each other's stories, and listen to God in prayer.

Sometimes as James leads the prayer on Saturday evenings, someone will spontaneously give thanks and praise for the way God has answered the prayers of God's people. Such expressions prompt all to rejoice in God's goodness, and their gratitude compels them to love as God loves. For those who attend Nampa Church, prayer has become a rhythm of communal life that both stimulates and perpetuates their common mission.

God's love cannot dwell in us if we are not practicing the hospitable discipline of prayer. Paul likened the sufferings of the present to the pains of childbirth. Even believers "groan inwardly while we wait for adoption, the redemption of our bodies" (Rom. 8:23b). The source of hope, Paul said, is that "the Spirit helps us in our weakness; for we do not know how to pray as we ought, but the very Spirit intercedes with sighs too deep for words" (Rom. 8:26). God answers these prayers in marvelous ways. "We know that all things work together for good for those who love God, who are called according to his purpose" (Rom. 8:28). Prayer creates the space for God to have God's way in the communal life of the church. It forms the two-way channel necessary for relationship.

Communication fuels relationship that generates love. The relationship between God and people rides on the rhythm of prayer as it creates the capacity for God to dwell in our midst. If we do not pray, we become malnourished. We lack ears to hear and eyes to see.

Prayer must become habit, a way of being. Friends who never connect through conversation are not really friends. Likewise, followers of God who never connect through prayer are not really followers. Waking up to God's presence means tuning-in: watching and listening for the times and places God's word appears in our world. This awakening is even brighter when mediated through the community of faith, a shared experience among God's people. We pray to welcome God's kingdom in our midst.

When You Pray, Move Your Feet

There is an old African proverb that says *When you pray, move your feet*. There will always be space for quiet, meditative, centering prayer. But if prayer is not prompting God's people to act, it is useless. Prayer fans into flame the mission of God's reconciliation on earth.

> *We pray, because Jesus taught us how to relocate our awareness of who God is and who we are (Matt. 6:9–14). We pray, because we need to experience the compassion of our heavenly parent. We pray, because it sharpens our intentions and makes us better listeners. We pray, because it heals us of blind unbelief and opens our eyes to God's will on earth. We pray, because we are never actually alone in this world. We pray, because we remember our true dependence when naming our daily needs: bread, forgiveness, peace with neighbors, and protection from trial. We pray, because we need help to see where the leavening yeast of God's grace is being kneaded into every nook and cranny of creation. We pray, so that when God's redemption is baked into our very lives and begins to rise throughout the world, we can share it with the hungry.*[2]

Benediction

> **May God, who always hears your prayers, awaken you to God's presence so that your feet become prayer**

in motion as you act justly, love mercy, and walk humbly with God.
Amen.

Exploration: Praying Together

∻ Pray the collect together.

∻ As you think about Rene, what contrast do you see between a woman who rarely made eye contact and one who rarely misses a meeting of The Living Room? How might this answer to prayer encourage someone like Monica?

∻ Read Acts 4:23–31. What do the disciples say about God in their prayer? What was the disciples' request?

∻ Describe a time when you or your missional community was re-aligned with God's mission through prayer.

∻ What comes to mind when you read that "prayer is waking up to the presence of God"? How might your missional community alter its rhythm to be awakened more fully?

∻ Pray together as a missional community, asking God to reveal God's will to you.

∻ Speak the benediction as a blessing to one another and as a call to action in God's mission.

Chapter 7

Words on the Way

Witnessing of God's Grace Together

ON EASTER SUNDAY, JIM SAT IN THE SANCTUARY OF CANAAN HILL Church going over the Psalm he would read later in the service. Others began to arrive. Jim greeted Danny as he came and sat down, and then Jim went back to his preparation. Jim looked up to see Hippie Mike come down the aisle to the pew where Danny waited for the service to begin. Jim smiled. Evidence of the grace of God sat side by side right there in this rural church building.

The first time Jim went to HideAway Lakes, the place where Danny and Hippie Mike live, he showed up just as a fight broke out. A woman yelled at Jim that he needed to get out of there; she then drove off in a hurry to call the sheriff. Jim turned to his friend with a what-do-we-do-now look. They had come to be a redemptive presence, so they continued on into the community. With knives slashing wildly, two groups of men yelled and lunged. Soon four sheriff cars came flying up the dirt road to break up yet another fight.

The original developers of HideAway Lakes envisioned a place where residents of Kansas City, one hour to the south, could go on weekends and holidays. Instead of hundreds of vacationers, now about fifty campsites have become the year-round home for a volatile mix of people. Substance abuse, violence, perversions — you find it all at HideAway Lakes. And kids. About forty children live there.

Jim originally went to HideAway Lakes to invite children to vacation Bible school. Relationships developed so that by the third year Canaan Hill Church decided to move its VBS to HideAway Lakes. They found it easier for congregational families to drive out than to transport all the children in. By this time the congregation regularly distributed food and clothes at HideAway Lakes and led Bible studies at the picnic pavilion near the entrance.

On one particular day, Danny sat in the pavilion with those who had gathered for the Bible study. Jim saw Hippie Mike's pickup coming down the road. Danny jumped up and headed for the truck. Jim looked at the other leader from Canaan Hill Church. They knew Hippie Mike and Danny had been on opposite sides in a recent fight. Both men started for the truck. While the other leader talked with Danny, Jim put his hand on Hippie's chest and urged him to back away. Everything got deathly quiet. Then Hippie Mike got in his truck and drove off.

Later everyone began to fully realize what happened in that moment. Over time the faithful presence of the people from Canaan Hill Church created trust among people who often find it difficult to have confidence in anyone. The persistence of that missional community to share freely the grace of God prompted those living in HideAway Lakes to pay attention. The quiet assurance of Jim and others brought calm to a community often overrun with violence.

On Easter, Danny and Hippie Mike greeted each other with a handshake during the passing of the peace. Then they went to the Communion Table together. With thanksgiving they heard again the good news: *brothers in Christ, your sins are forgiven.*

Collect

> *God of resplendent holiness and iridescent grace,*
> *Whose Light conquered the darkness of death;*
> *Cleanse and enliven our hearts so completely*

That we may fully proclaim your goodness in word
and deed;
To our Savior and Lord be glory forever.
Amen.

Stories for the Journey

Cleopas and another person, possibly his wife, left Jerusalem for their home in Emmaus. As they started the seven-mile journey, the bewilderment of the previous three days immersed their conversation in more doubt than assurance. They had watched Jesus die on the cross. They knew the location of the garden tomb in which Joseph had placed Jesus' body. But on this morning, with women making outrageous claims and disciples running back and forth, the news spread that only angels inhabited the burial place. The disciples searched for definitive responses to the cascade of questions that poured over them.

As the two disciples trudged toward Emmaus, a fellow traveler stepped in cadence beside them. Only later did the two realize their companion was Jesus. The interchange between Jesus and the disciples reveals key elements in being a witness of God's grace.

The two disciples talked about God while they were *on the way* home. Deeply ingrained in Jewish life, this practice came from a portion of the *Shema*: "Keep these words that I am commanding you today in your heart. Recite them to your children and talk about them when you are at home and when you are away, when you lie down and when you rise" (Deut. 6:6–7). This formed a standard practice for people of faith.

The two travelers welcomed the third person to join them. After arriving in Emmaus, they invited their new acquaintance to stay for a meal. This is *hospitality*, creating space that allows another person to join the conversation (see chapter 9).

Luke's telling of this story reveals careful *listening*. Jesus asked a question. Cleopas responded with a question. Jesus asked for clarification even though he already knew the answer. Jesus listened as these disciples reiterated the confusing narrative.

In recent decades, some have tried to reduce the gospel to bullet points or a script used in evangelism. The examples of witness in the Gospels and the Acts of the Apostles involve *stories*. The disciples told their traveling companion the story of Jesus. They spoke in narrative, not propositions. The Jewish leaders tried to silence Peter and John. These men, who talked and ate with Jesus after the resurrection, said, "We cannot keep from speaking about what we have seen and heard" (Acts 4:20). Peter and John witnessed of the risen Lord by telling stories. In fact, we know about the resurrection solely because of testimony. We rely on the stories, not video clips or DNA samples.

Faithful witness requires *theological reflection* on what is observed. After Jesus listened to Cleopas describe the events of the previous days, "beginning with Moses and all the Prophets, [Jesus] explained to them what was said in all the Scriptures concerning himself" (Luke 24:27 NIV). *You see this?* Jesus said. *This is that.* Jesus placed the current experiences in the trajectory of God's mission as revealed in the Law and the Prophets.

"When [Jesus] was at the table with them, he took bread, gave thanks, broke it and began to give it to them. Then their eyes were opened and they recognized him, and he disappeared from their sight. They asked each other, 'Were not our hearts burning within us while he talked with us on the road and opened the Scriptures to us?'" (Luke 24:30–32). Those yet to choose to follow the Savior will see Jesus in the hospitality showed them by the church. There they find a place to ask their questions, and then hear the stories about the God who deeply loves all of creation. And God's kingdom will come on earth.

Ready to Listen

Faith and religion became privatized in the last half of the twentieth century in the United States. The cultural concept of live-and-let-live asserted that a person should go through life without interruption from outside sources. Some persons insisted that this must include silence concerning all things of the spiritual dimension. That concept pushes against the biblical practices of talking about the things of God *in the midst* of everyday life. When considering witnessing of God's grace, the person of faith will find natural ways to point out God's involvement in our world while engaged in even the most mundane of tasks.

Hospitality sets the table for meaningful conversation. In our mediated world with people increasingly connected through smartphones, tablets, and computers, people still need the face-to-face relationship. Welcome and kindness warm the air in which the most important things in life can be discussed. Transformation happens in that kind of relationship. Henri Nouwen wrote, "Hospitality is not to change people, but to offer them space where change can take place."[1] The context in which witness occurs will involve hospitality.

For the person who witnesses to God's grace, hospitality invites the other person to speak. That requires careful *listening*. There will come a time to speak, but that moment can be discerned only by listening. The witness will listen well to the person speaking. But the witness will also be sensitive to the guidance of the Holy Spirit.

Sometimes testimonies involve extensive personal stories of spiritual experiences. This type of testimony is incomplete. The witness the world needs to hear involves *telling God's story*. John stated that he had a broad catalog of stories about Jesus to draw from in writing his gospel. The stories he selected were intentional, "that you may come to believe that Jesus is the Messiah" (John 20:31). Witness involves using sights and smells and dialogue and feelings that show God at work.

The witness who effectively tells God's story will help others locate their stories in the trajectory of God's mission. Involvement in the community of Jesus' followers creates the environment where the community learns to recognize God at work. Through prayer and reflection, the community discerns how God's grace is evident in their part of the world. Through Bible study they learn how God worked in the past, then they begin to see the arc from

New Testament times through the history of the church up to the present day. In worship they learn a vocabulary that equips them to speak about God beyond the church. Witness involves looking at the present through the lens provided by *theological reflection*.

Eager to Speak

God has called us to speak words of hope. Peter urged Christians facing obstacles and trials to always be ready to speak of the hope they had because of Jesus. And "do it with gentleness and reverence," he added (1 Pet. 3:15–16). Their actions would verify the truth they declared. In speaking words of hope, we witness to the God of hope.

God has called us to love and work for peace. Jesus said, "Blessed are the peacemakers, for they will be called children of God" (Matt. 5:9). In pursuing peace, we witness to the God of peace.

God has called us to freely love everyone: God, neighbor, and enemy. The world will know Jesus as the Messiah, the one anointed and sent by God, as they see the great love expressed by the Christians. In acts of love, we witness to the God of love.

May our words, pursuits, and acts witness to the abundant life offered by God through Jesus.

Benediction

May God, who is always with us, make you a
courageous witness in word and deed so that the
world will receive the good news that God's kingdom
has come and Jesus reigns as King.
Amen.

Exploration: Witnessing of God's Grace Together

❧ Pray the collect together.

❧ What emotions would you use to describe the before and after in the relationship between Danny and Hippie Mike? Describe a time when you experienced the type of emotion that accompanies God's goodness.

❧ Describe a time when you gained great insight while *on the way* with other pilgrims.

❧ Retell a Bible story that has been formative in your spiritual journey. What does the story reveal about God? About God's will for us?

❧ Theology literally means "words about God." Anyone who speaks words about God is a theologian. How might your missional community better articulate its discernment of God in your midst (theological reflection)?

❧ Read 1 Peter 3:13–16. How can you more effectively explain the hope Christians have because of Jesus? What will give your missional community greater courage in its witness?

❧ Speak the benediction as a blessing to one another and as a call to action in God's mission.

Part III

Catholic

The church participates in God's mission by proclaiming *to the whole world — all classes and cultures, all ages and genders, all nationalities and races —* that God is holy love and, through Jesus, God is transforming a people who embody that holy love as empowered and knit together by the Holy Spirit, a sign that the kingdom of God is here.

Ecclesial Practices

Offering Hospitality Together

Living Simply and Generously Together

Confronting Evil and Injustice Together

Galatians 3:23–29

Now before faith came, we were imprisoned and guarded under the law until faith would be revealed. Therefore the law was our disciplinarian until Christ came, so that we might be justified by faith. But now that faith has come, we are no longer subject to a disciplinarian, for in Christ Jesus you are all children of God through faith. As many of you as were baptized into Christ have clothed yourselves with Christ. There is no longer Jew or Greek, there is no longer slave or free, there is no longer male and female; for all of you are one in Christ Jesus. And if you belong to Christ, then you are Abraham's offspring, heirs according to the promise.

Chapter 8

Catholic Church

Galatians 3:23–29

PAUL WAS SHAKEN WHEN HE WROTE TO THE CONGREGATIONS HE planted in Galatia. He loved these people. In a season when he was too ill to continue his missionary journey, they nursed him back to health even before they shared a common faith. The Galatians responded to the message of Christ he preached by trusting that Jesus was the Messiah.

After Paul's departure, other missionaries with conflicting requirements for salvation preached that the Galatians must be circumcised to be included in God's family. The young converts were keen to follow through even if surgery was what it took. Paul minced no words:

> *You foolish Galatians! Who has bewitched you? . . . The only thing I want to learn from you is this: Did you receive the Spirit by doing the works of the law or by believing what you heard? Are you so foolish? Having started with the Spirit, are you now ending with the flesh? Did you experience so much for nothing? (Gal. 3:1–4a).*

In an effort to convince the Galatians of their newfound freedom, Paul wrote that Christ's gospel does not include the former administrative restrictions of the law. *Your freedom really is free,* he said, *and what is more: all previous lines drawn in the sand between ethnicities, socioeconomic divisions, and gender identities have disappeared.*

That's good news! In Christ all previous boundaries for defining earth's family no longer applied. Paul held nothing back in this letter. Over-and-against no longer defined God's people. The once-for-all gospel event of Christ's life, death, and resurrection shattered all barriers to adoption into God's universal family.

In the old country, the law protected segregation of the chosen people from outsiders. But in Christ, separation is abolished. In the economy of the region of Galatia, the freedom of folks in charge depended on the enslavement of others. But in Christ, there is no such thing as master and slave. Cultural assumptions for the Galatians demanded that gender roles enforce an inescapable power dynamic. But in Christ, gender is no longer grounds for exclusion.

You have put on an entirely new identity, the missionary told his converts. *You are nothing like you used to be!* This new identity was not conferred by religious ritual or surgical proof, but by the reception of the gift of God's Spirit. Baptism dramatizes the story of salvation, but is not a magical formula for reconciliation. Everyone who believes in Jesus by faith is a child of God and a rightful heir of God's promises. God's reign of love is lived on a level plane and no one is left out based on culture, economics, or gender.

There are no second-class citizens in God's family, Paul insisted. God's promise belonged equally to the Galatians as it did to the Jews, the slave and the free, male and female. The promises of God have no limit. They are universal.

Collect

> *Our gracious host,*
> *Who calls all people to sit at the heavenly banquet*
> *table;*
> *Cause us to hear anew your promise to our Father*
> *Abraham*

*So that all people on earth shall be blessed with your
    divine favor;*
*For the sake of our Lord Jesus Christ, who lives and
    reigns with you and the Holy Spirit, one God,
    forever and ever.*
Amen.

One Big, Happy Family

God's church is catholic. The word *catholic* means "universal," which indicates that the church's doors are open to anyone who receives the inherited gift of God's Spirit, that is, salvation found in Christ. You do not have to be Jewish, Galatian, Roman, Congolese, or Malaysian. You do not have to be rich and famous or poor and hungry. You may be male or female. All you need is adoption into God's family. How? According to Paul's letter to the Galatians, by belonging to Christ's body (the church) symbolized by the ritual of baptism, believing the salvation of God, and becoming God's children.

Paul described the tension between law and faith diversely throughout the letters exchanged with congregations he nurtured in the Christian faith. He depicted the law as an administrative guardian, a "protective custody, so to speak, until the way of faith was revealed" (Gal. 3:23 NLT). When the Galatians came to know life in Christ, they did not carry forward the same attachment to the law that the Jews did. Christ's salvation is a liberating gift, Paul said, a vast inheritance into which everyone can be graciously adopted. When rival missionaries threatened this inheritance through their conflicting message, Paul reacted strongly. They entirely missed the point of the good news when they said the Galatians must revert to an old requirement of the law — that is, circumcision — to be fully included.

The missionary Paul dug into Jewish history to support his argument. The Law came *after* God's promise to Abraham as a way to keep the promise intact. God promised Abraham that a lasting relationship shared with Abraham's family would bless *all nations*. Simply keeping the Law could not claim the promise. Originally received through Jewish ancestry and obedience, the promise became available later through Gentile adoption and participation. Paul insisted that law and promise do not conflict with each other because the law is not the source of life. God is.

For a period in history, the law guarded the life-giving promises of God, but it was by no means the source. Jesus the Christ blew open the restrictions of the law to induce God's reign of love, administrated by nothing less than the Holy Spirit. When God's Spirit filled the believers at Pentecost, the embryonic church became a worldwide force.

Being set free in Christ was like passing from childhood into adulthood, from dependency to interdependent responsibility. Freedom in Christ was not a license to foolhardy lawlessness, but rather a reorientation under a new promise in a brand new epoch.

Paul went so far as to say that the law served its purpose. The promise to Abraham through the gift of the Spirit expressed in the unifying waters of baptism is what delineates God's family, not the law. "But now that faith has come," Paul said, "we are no longer subject to a disciplinarian, for in Christ Jesus you are all children of God through faith" (Gal. 3:25–26).

Ethnicity, socioeconomic status, and gender have nothing to do with adoption into God's family. All dividing lines in the human family are null and void. Assurance of inclusion cannot be found in adherence to exclusive rules, but by belonging to Christ. *You are in!* Paul declared to the Galatians. *You belong!*

The three distinctions Paul declared void cover common human divisions: ethnic, socioeconomic, and gender. At no time in life can anyone fully escape these labels. But in Christ, everyone who believes also belongs. No one is excluded. In Christ, the circumstances of birth and social standing mean nothing. Grace triumphs over classism, ethnocentricity, and gender oppression.

According to the Nicene Creed, a signifying mark of the church is its catholicity. God's family spans the globe, including every human who chooses adoption as God intended in the beginning.

Catholicity in Motion

When God's universal church practices hospitality together (see chapter 9), the diverse members who belong to Christ's body begin to understand that there is no longer Jew or Gentile. Former racial and ethnic dividing lines cease to matter. God shows no partiality to those God loves and serves, and neither should those who are "united with Christ in baptism" (Gal. 3:27). We all breathe, we all thirst, we all bleed. When offering hospitality and meeting the basic needs of both insiders and outsiders in God's church, the universal body recognizes it is our humanity we share in common.

When God's universal church practices the rhythm of living simply and generously (see chapter 10), the church leans into God's generous salvation available to all people. For too many persons, someone exerts control over them, often denying free access to available resources. In contrast, the reaching-out fellowship of God's people freely shares whatever they have with anyone in need. When the church considers itself universal, each person becomes a sibling to be provided for and protected.

When God's universal church confronts evil and injustice (see chapter 11), there are no longer grounds for status divisions or oppression of fellow human beings. An example would be gender inequality that has plagued the human family since the fall of Adam and Eve in the garden. In Christ such distinction dissolves on the basis of full and equal access to God's promises. Injustice will be overcome as the church embodies its freedom in Christ.

Families do not Discriminate

Family photos are a precious sight to behold when one or more of the siblings are obviously not biological. Perhaps you have adopted children, or been the adopted, or know friends who have or are. We are all adopted into God's family. God delights in our collective family photo that is dynamic with the colors, stories, and perspectives we each bring to the picture.

The practice of circumcision, a ritual for men only, would have grossly divided the newly universal body of Christ. In the waters of baptism there is neither Jew nor Greek, slave nor free, male and female. Everyone of us who goes down into the water is raised to new life, donning a new wardrobe in Christ. Anyone who believes, anyone adopted into God's family and belonging to Christ, becomes an heir to God's promises.

> *The church participates in God's mission by proclaiming to the whole world — all classes and cultures, all ages and genders, all nationalities and races — that God is holy love and, through Jesus, God is transforming a people who embody that holy love as empowered and knit together by the Holy Spirit, a sign that the kingdom of God is here.*

God offers life to all who come in repentance (2 Pet. 3:9), *all classes and cultures, all ages and genders, all nationalities and races.* Baptismal waters do not discriminate. Neither does God and, therefore, neither should the universal church.

Benediction

> *May God, who adopted you into God's family and gave you an entirely new wardrobe in faith, cause you to live triumphantly as an heir to the glorious promise of God in Christ to be a blessing to the ends of the earth.*
> *Amen.*

Exploration: Catholic Church

❧ Pray the collect together.

❧ Are you adopted, have you adopted children, or do you know someone who is or has? What stories can you tell about that experience or process? How does this inform your understanding of being adopted into God's family?

❧ Why do you think humans have typically subdivided into ethnic, cultural, or socioeconomic strata by identifying themselves as different from "the other"?

❧ Read Galatians 3:23–29. What happens in the reign of God, inaugurated in Jesus and empowered by the Spirit, to the typical dividing walls?

❧ Why would those who crafted the Nicene Creed consider catholicity as one of the four most important characteristics of the church?

❧ What might it look like for your missional community to embody the inclusive nature of the gospel more fully? What might you adjust? What practices might you add?

❧ Speak the benediction as a blessing to one another and as a call to action in God's mission.

Chapter 9

Strangers Becoming Friends

Offering Hospitality Together

THE LIGHTS DANCED AS THEY REFLECTED OFF THE TINSEL AND OR-
naments adorning the prominently displayed Christmas
tree. A table containing a magnificent and diverse spread of
holiday food and beverages graced the center of the room. Laughter
and music filled the air. Greeters stood at the entrance, ready to
welcome the evening's guests. On a cold December night, powerful
warmth emanated from the building when Lowell Church hosted
dozens of local foster families for a festive Christmas party held
in their honor.

The building buzzed with excitement as nearly 80 children and
120 adults attended the party while volunteers from Lowell Church
and the larger community served the guests. Children visited craft
stations where they constructed colorful holiday creations to take
home. Parents and chaperones connected with one another and
found encouragement by sharing stories of their foster parenting
journey. The highlight of the evening for everyone was the arrival
of Santa Claus who came bearing gifts for each child. The joy of
the Christmas season permeated the entire evening.

This event, which has become an annual tradition, is one of
the few environments where kids and adults involved in foster
care find a safe place to be themselves. At the party they realize that everyone present understands their situation. And the

people of Lowell Church have been sensitive. Instead of seizing the party as a photo op, they view the event as a simple extension of hospitality.

The Christmas party was the dream of a handful of people including Joanne, a Department of Children and Families Supervisor and longtime member of Lowell Church. The former pastor, Jeff, was also instrumental in planting seeds for a ministry to these families to later develop and grow under the leadership of John, the current pastor.

Foster care is a passionate calling for Jeff and his wife Kelley, who have welcomed several displaced children into their own home throughout the years. When Jeff was the pastor of Lowell Church, his family would often show up to worship with a new child or teenager. The congregation unconditionally embraced these children as family. This warm welcome provided the children a refuge, a place where they were free from being treated as a possession.

Jeff and Kelley desire to be a living illustration of hospitality. Their example has helped inspire dozens of people in the missional communities they have served to give gifts to foster children at Christmas or volunteer with nonprofit organizations that help connect siblings in foster care. A handful of their close friends have even chosen to become foster parents themselves. They, along with many others in the foster care community, have embraced the vocation of treating every child as their own.

Many of the children who have walked through the doors of Lowell Church have a past that is marked by cycles of poverty and substance and sexual abuse. This congregation has sought to offer an alternative narrative to these children, one marked by warmth, love, and nurture. From the weekly practice of initially welcoming children in the care of Jeff and Kelley's family to the annual Christmas party for area foster families, Lowell Church has learned what it means to embody the spiritual discipline of hospitality.

Collect

Welcoming God,
Who opens wide the door to the down and out, the
*   broken and neglected;*
Help us find your face in the stranger and newcomer,
So that your loving embrace may be extended to them
*   through us, your people;*
In gratitude to the Good Shepherd who provides and
*   protects.*
Amen.

Welcoming the Stranger

The ancient Near East in which Jesus lived viewed hospitality to strangers as one of the highest virtues. Welcoming a desperate traveler in what were often harsh, desert conditions meant providing necessary food, precious life-sustaining water, and protection from danger. Hospitality in this culture was not merely a kind thing to do but often a matter of life or death.

The biblical tradition upholds and expands the practice of hospitality as a means of honoring the Lord and loving one's neighbor. Widows, orphans, the poor, and foreigners represented the land's most vulnerable people and were to be the recipients of hospitality by God's people. Hospitality to the sojourner was woven into the Levitical law and grounded in the character of God. "The alien who resides with you shall be to you as the citizen among you; you shall love the alien as yourself, for you were aliens in the land of Egypt: I am the Lord your God" (Lev. 19:34). The prophet Isaiah made hospitality an issue of justice, weaving together piety and action by suggesting that true fasting included the desire to "share your bread with the hungry, and bring the homeless poor into your house; when you see the naked, to cover them" (Is. 58:7).

According to Jesus' teaching in Matthew 25, hospitality has eternal significance. When we stand before God's throne in judgment, Jesus said, we won't be required to take a doctrinal quiz or quote a series of memorized Scriptures. We won't be asked if we prayed a particular prayer. Instead, one of the questions we will face centers around our extension of hospitality to the *least of these*. Did we see the face of Christ in strangers and invite them in? Did we visit the sick and imprisoned? Clothe the naked? Feed the hungry?

Jesus modeled this kind of radical welcome in his own ministry by frequently crossing commonly accepted boundaries to share meals with "the other." Early Christians followed the example of their Lord and made the meal a hallmark of their gatherings. People from various races and classes were welcomed around one table. Congregational leaders were to be hospitable and "well thought of by outsiders" (1 Tim. 3:2, 7). Believers were encouraged to practice hospitality because in welcoming strangers they believed that "some have entertained angels without knowing it" (Heb. 13:2).

In many developed nations, the idea of hospitality as warmly receiving the stranger is often lost. Instead, it is replaced by the notion of the hospitality industry, a commercial practice intended to cultivate relationships that are mutually beneficial. But Jesus challenged hospitality based on reciprocity by saying, "But when you give a banquet, invite the poor, the crippled, the lame, and the blind. And you will be blessed, because they cannot repay you, for you will be repaid at the resurrection of the righteous" (Luke 14:13–14).

Hospitality cannot be boiled down to a simple list of tasks done for certain people who can serve you in return. Nor is the mission of the church to be welcoming just so that it will attract people. Genuine hospitality, grounded in the hospitality of God, must flow outward with the simple intention of inviting strangers to become friends.

Nurturing Relationships

Hospitality is the spiritual discipline of creating space for people with no expectation of repayment. This ecclesial practice includes opening the doors wide without predetermining who may walk through them. More than welcoming someone to an event or a program, it involves opening our lives to the prospect of new relationships. Missional communities committed to offering hospitality must be prepared to take relational risks.

The dinner table provides a sacred place where warmth and nourishment are often experienced and people are initiated into the life of the kingdom of God. The practice of consistently sharing meals can have a transformative effect on a community. This truly becomes a missional practice when the table is intentionally extended to include new people.

Discovery Church decided to move their Sunday morning gathering outside of the church building in response to a need to provide a weekend meal for their community's homeless. Out of this experience emerged the desire to begin a communal breakfast and lunch program for the homeless and underfed. Those involved spoke passionately about how it was more than just providing food but involved knowing their neighbors and being known. Hospitable, mission-shaped communities recognize that shared bread leads to shared life.

The language we use is a critical factor in creating a hospitable community. Do we inappropriately use language of "us" and "them" that immediately excludes? Or is our language warm and inviting to newcomers? In our community's worship do we use language and liturgy that is inclusive? Is insider talk either eliminated or explained when necessary? In all formal and informal gatherings as well as in printed and web-based communication, vibrant missional communities will tend to ask, *How will the newcomer experience this? How might he or she be able to participate and belong in a meaningful way?*

Hospitality is about receiving as well as giving. One congregation whose demographic was historically Caucasian began seeing an increased number of Asian guests in its worship services as a result of an effective English language ministry. Congregational leaders asked their newest members for help to teach the congregation about Asian culture. The United States flag was removed from the worship space to stress the universality of the body of Christ.

The result consisted of more than a congregation offering a warm welcome to foreigners. The community truly became multicultural, reflecting the beautiful tapestry of God's kingdom.

Unfortunately, for some congregations hospitality is limited to having clear signage in a building, friendly greeters, and good coffee. While these things are helpful, hospitality must go beyond welcoming people who come to us. Offering hospitality involves an active process. Missional communities will constantly ask themselves, *In whom do we see the face of Jesus?* When the answer comes, they ask, *How can we welcome this person as we would Jesus?*

Water and Spirit

One of the most powerful metaphors in the New Testament is of the church as the family of God. When we consider that the gospel crosses lines of race, gender, culture, economic status, and nationality, this becomes a transformative image. The church is called to practice familial love: welcoming the fatherless, the stranger, and the disenfranchised. The family of God reaches out and invites those who seek a spiritual home.

Missional communities understand that relationship with God's family consists not of bloodline but rather new birth through water and the Spirit (John 3:5). As the Lowell Church story illustrates, family is less about physical birth and more about the people in whom you choose to invest.

The words hospital and hospitality share the same root. Both have to do with welcoming guests and providing shelter and care for those in need. God calls the church to create space for the healing of individuals and communities: physically, spiritually, emotionally, and relationally.

Benediction

> *May God, who graciously welcomes all people with open arms, enlarge your heart so you can warmly*

receive in the name of Christ those in need of refuge, shelter, and care.
Amen.

Exploration: Offering Hospitality Together

❧ Pray the collect together.

❧ Imagine standing in the corner watching the foster families at the Christmas party. What do you think may have been going through the hearts and minds of the adults? The children? The volunteers?

❧ Read Luke 7:36–39. Jesus practiced radical hospitality to those on the margins of society. How did Jesus' treatment of others affect religious leaders of his day? What does the response Jesus received suggest about the challenges your missional community may experience if it practices hospitality in the same way?

❧ Read 1 Peter 4:8–11. What are the characteristics of a hospitable community?

❧ Compile a list of groups or persons in your community for whom an extension of hospitality is greatly needed. List some ideas that your missional community could explore for engaging each group.

❧ Speak the benediction as a blessing to one another and as a call to action in God's mission.

Chapter 10

Grace, Fellowship, and Service

Living Simply and Generously Together

THE NEW BEGINNINGS CONGREGATION ERUPTED WITH SHOUTS AND clapping at the announcement; they had an offer. As required by the congregation's bylaws, a congregational meeting to sell their facility would be held on a subsequent Sunday.

Within three months of becoming the pastor of New Beginnings Church, Shane realized that the congregation faced mammoth financial challenges. Forty-one percent of their income went to service the mortgage when he arrived. When the congregation launched the building program three years before, the indebtedness they took on was 617 percent of the total monies raised the previous year. Finance professionals usually recommend that a mortgage not exceed 200 to 300 percent. With a new pastor leading them, the congregation set out to fill the seats with employed, middle-class families who could help pay the bills.

But a growing discontent set in. Since the congregation had ignored the wisdom of Proverbs 22:7, "the borrower is the slave of the lender," it could not follow the example of Jesus and give itself away. Shane shared with the church board his growing frustration and angst. Led by a vocal minority, the board dismissed their pastor's concern. The board insisted that they must keep the building, even though it meant the loss of staff members and few funds for ministries.

Shane resigned. He felt shame because they failed to raise adequate funds. But those feelings paled in comparison when he realized that they had distorted the gospel they claimed to proclaim. He repented.

The congregation did too. Some board members left when the congregation insisted on righting the listing ship. The congregation called Shane a second time to serve as the pastor of New Beginnings Church. Before committing to a new relationship, church leaders and Shane drafted a vision statement that guided the process forward, especially concerning their debilitating debt. They started praying with fervor each Sunday, "Forgive us our debts."

The congregation erupted with giddy excitement when they realized that God had answered their prayers. The congregation voted unanimously to sell their facility. A second ballot was distributed concerning the purchase of a new meeting place for the congregation. In their search, they wanted to be in a neighborhood where they could be a faithful presence of God's grace and they could add beauty. They found an old strip mall strategically located in their city, near a high school and two parks. The journey of this missional community continues unencumbered by the weight of debt.

Collect

> *O gracious God,*
> *Who never falters in providing bountiful gifts to all of*
>   *creation;*
> *Cause us to be a people who receive your goodness*
>   *with thanksgiving*
> *So that we may cheerfully share your blessings with*
>   *others;*
> *To you be glory in and through the church.*
> *Amen.*

Without Folds

Paul said, "He that giveth, let him do it with simplicity" (Rom. 12:8 KJV). Other translations use the word generosity instead of simplicity. The Greek word (*haplotētos*) used in Romans 12:8 and other places has the root meaning of singleness. The literal image is something without folds. Current idioms that get at this idea include saying that there are no strings attached or WYSIWYG (What You See Is What You Get). Paul urged the Roman congregation to give without an agenda hidden in the folds.

This word also carries the notion of sincerity (see Col. 3:22). As the concept of generosity comes into focus, then, we see that it is about a wholesome attitude and a right spirit more than the size of the gift.

Paul told his friends in Corinth about the liberality of the Macedonians and urged them to give freely for the needs of their brothers and sisters in Jerusalem. Generosity overflowed from the simplicity of the Macedonians. They had a sincere concern for the well-being of God's people. Their concern expressed itself in uncomplicated and uncalculated giving.

The Macedonian congregations pleaded with Paul for the "privilege of sharing in this service" (2 Cor. 8:4 NIV). In this phrase Paul used forms of three words with deep theological meaning: *charis* or grace, *koinonia* or sharing through community, and *diakonia* or service. The Macedonians begged Paul to allow them to graciously live as a community of service. That, Paul said, exemplified generosity.

Paul used the word "grace" (*charis*) ten times in 2 Corinthians 8 and 9. Grace sets the tone of this passage when Paul said that the grace of God becomes visible through overflowing generosity. Since the Macedonians gave beyond their means, only God's grace could adequately describe the source of their liberality.

The Macedonian congregations faced the outside pressure of living in a culture hostile to Christ. This brought severe affliction to these people. But the simplicity of their giving testified to the reality that they did not do so because of outside pressure. The generosity Paul described in this passage did not come from external compulsion. Reluctance to share freely comes from outside pressure forcing persons to do what they do not want to do. In contrast, Paul urged the Corinthians to find the joy that comes from voluntary, inside-out giving for the benefit of others. Paul described giving as an organic revelation of grace. Through simple generosity the church gives itself as a means of God's grace.

The kind of giving Paul envisioned occurs within the fellowship (*koinonia*) of the church. Paul did not have charity in mind where one who has gives to one who does not have. This type of hierarchy does not fit the concept embodied in the word *koinonia*. Instead, Paul described an openhanded living that naturally dwells in the giving and receiving of a community.

The congregations shared a common life with God. They also shared a common life with each other. Paul reported his solidarity with the Macedonian congregations. Paul told the Corinthians that the generosity that emerged from their *koinonia* would bring glory to God. Through simple generosity the church embodies the incarnate Word known by its sacrificial giving.

Generous living, Paul said, involves energetic serving (*diakonia*). When James and John asked Jesus for a privileged position in the kingdom of God, Jesus told them, "Whoever wishes to become great among you must be your servant (*diakonos*)" (Mark 10:43). God blesses with abundance, Paul said to the Corinthians, so they must "share abundantly in every good work" (2 Cor. 9:8).

Sharing generously expresses thanksgiving to God, so un-calculated giving is a form of worship. The writer of Hebrews noted that sometimes worship is expressed as exaltation of God, "a sacrifice of praise to God." Other times the sacrifices "pleasing to God" involve intentional efforts "to do good and to share what you have" (Heb. 13:15, 16). Simple generosity initiates service as an expression of praise to God and prompts others to join in expressing thanksgiving for God's gifts.

Simple generosity, then, entails God's grace flowing in and through the common life of God's people for the common good of all God's creation. *Charis* and *koinonia* and *diakonia*, three in one. Simple. Generous.

The Sparkle of Simplicity

Attempts to package Paul's concept of generosity into a program-in-a-box will fail spectacularly. What Paul described as simple suggests that generosity cannot be folded into booklets or displayed as posters and video clips. The simple generosity Paul proposed comes forth as a missional community steps into the flow of God's grace. The community's participation in what God has already begun through grace shapes the community so that expressions of generosity emerge out of its very being as the body of Christ.

A missional community can intentionally nurture the kind of openness to God and each other from which generosity can take root and grow. The ecclesial practices we discuss, for example, when engaged in by a missional community will shape it in ways that make open-handed living a natural expression of *charis* and *koinonia* and *diakonia*. The spiritual practices of prayer (chapter 6), Bible study (chapter 13), receiving the sacraments (chapter 14), and worship (chapter 19) serve as a means of grace by which God shapes "a peculiar people" (1 Pet. 1:9 KJV). The ministries of hospitality (chapter 9) and confronting injustice (chapter 11) provide specific contexts in which a missional community can share freely. The three key theological terms Paul used in 2 Corinthians 8:4 each connect with a specific ecclesial practice: discerning God's grace (chapter 5), nurturing the sharing-out community (chapter 17), and compassionate service (chapter 18). Intentional engagement of these ecclesial practices will shape a missional community in ways that help the body of Christ naturally express itself in generosity.

A key element in becoming a generous people involves the biblical concept of simplicity in giving. Giving "without folds" means that generosity is not a dollar bill used in a fanciful origami creation. Complicated steps are not required; generosity just places the gift in the hands of another person.

The evangelical church in the United States has been sidetracked by its methods in recent decades. Some congregations, for example, believe that they must have a designated game room to effectively reach the youth of their city. So they pour tens of thousands of dollars into their "if we build it they will come" dreams. Some church planters hear that they must fully utilize social media if their enterprise will take flight. In both cases, proponents will claim that the facility and Internet presence are tools through which they intend to build relationships with people who need to be nurtured in their spiritual lives. Unfortunately, in too many cases the pastors and missionaries have morphed into facility managers and entrepreneurs. Instead of direct engagement in redemptive activities, they mediate those impulses in ways that costs money, takes time, and ultimately leads them off course. The methods end up sapping energy from the mission because of a growing complexity.

A missional community will engage directly in its ministry of reconciliation, using all available resources, but not getting distracted into thinking that keeping the resources well-tuned is the primary goal. The simplicity of unmediated ministry, the person-to-person, face-to-face interaction Jesus demonstrated, leads to generous expressions of God's grace.

From the Same Cloth

The transition for New Beginnings Church has just begun. They have already formed partnerships with other groups living in the pattern of the kingdom of God who share the new space. They developed a financial plan that makes the facility self-sustaining; all ministries that use the facility will do so rent-free. The oppressive debt turned the congregation into slaves in exile. Paying off the mortgage released the congregation from bondage so that it now can authentically live out the gospel of Jesus Christ. A simplified life means they can fully engage directly in God's mission.

Simplicity and generosity come from the same cloth. The transparency and sincerity of one fosters the lavishness of the other. Both contribute to the missional community being shaped as the body of Christ out of which naturally flows the extravagance of God's goodness.

Benediction

May God, who gives bountiful gifts to all of creation,
shower you with the goodness of love and peace
so that your thankfulness can be expressed with
generous expressions of kindness and mercy.
Amen.

Exploration: Living Simply and Generously Together

❧ Pray the collect together.

❧ The people of New Beginnings Church rejoiced when they broke the chains of debt. Describe a time when you felt freed from a heavy load (financial, emotional, relational, or other).

❧ Read 2 Corinthians 8:1–5. Describe the connection between grace (*charis*) and generosity. Between fellowship or sharing (*koinonia*) and generosity. Between service (*diakonia*) and generosity.

❧ What are some areas of your life as a missional community that may need to be "unfolded" or simplified so you can better embody and proclaim the gospel? What steps will move your community toward that simplification?

❧ Where do you see God's grace at work in your immediate cultural context but beyond your missional community? Describe characteristics of the missional community best shaped to join what God has started. What ecclesial practices will form you as that kind of people?

❧ Speak the benediction as a blessing to one another and as a call to action in God's mission.

Chapter 11

Justice for All

Confronting Evil and Injustice Together

SHY AND PERHAPS A LITTLE SCARED, THIRTY-EIGHT TEENAGE GIRLS poured into the church building in their neighborhood with the promise of a glamour makeover and personalized photo shoot. Like other teenage girls, the idea of getting dolled up for the camera sent a thrill up their spines. But these girls were not exactly like other girls their age. By accident of birth they existed in vulnerable situations, at risk for lives of pain and oppression. Their reality consisted of instability and food insecurity at the mild end of the spectrum and abuse and human trafficking at the harsh end. Day-to-day reality was laced with the fearful fight to survive. At the Dress for Freedom event, the message that all human beings are created beautiful and whole enveloped their vulnerability.

Invited to a day of pampering, girls from the lowest-income and highest-crime neighborhood in Portland, Oregon, received the tender care of nearly one hundred volunteers from a variety of congregations. Stations set up throughout the church building sent the girls to get their nails, hair, and makeup done; to create their own jewelry; to a dress rack to select formal attire for the photo-shoot; and, of course, to the photographer's station to have their portraits made.

In the midst of nail polish and curling irons, the giggling and spoiling was put on pause for a while. Event organizers gathered the special guests for a message from two women whose stories captivated their imaginations. The speakers were not unlike the guests of honor. Their stories originated in pain and vulnerability, descended into darkness and abuse, and ended with the rescue of God's love. The message resonated deeply in the hearts of the teenagers: God's love is lavish, no matter who we are and where we came from.

The teens were overcome. With tears streaming down their faces, they raced forward to hug the speakers. Somewhat bewildered by the reality that they were not alone, some of these girls were hearing for the first time of a God who loved them enough to rescue them.

In the years of the first decade of the new millennium, Clear Creek Church was much like many other well-intentioned congregations: full of loving, caring Christians who were comfortable doing ministry for ministry's sake. There was no sense of urgency for reaching beyond themselves. When Pastor Gary caught sight of God's vision of turning the congregation inside out for the sake of God's justice-mission, things began to change. A series of compassion outreach events compelled the congregation beyond the four walls of their church building. Slowly, the people of Clear Creek realized that God's church does not have a mission; God's mission has a church. They were called to help accomplish that mission.

Because of the faithfulness of its leaders to listen to the Scriptures and to ask what it means to be God's people, Clear Creek has become a centrifugal force for confronting the evil of human trafficking in one of the biggest ports for slavery in the United States. The Dress for Freedom event is just one example of the myriad of ways Clear Creek directly confronted the injustice of human trafficking on their home turf.

Collect

> *God of compassionate justice,*
> *Who jealously seeks the abolition of every enemy of*
> *your reign of love;*

Draw us so close to your heart
That ours beats in tandem with your desire for the end
of evil;
May your kingdom come, your will be done here on
earth as it is in heaven.
Amen.

More than Conquerors

Given the choice, God chooses justice over ceremonial worship every day of the week. God cares only about the kind of religiosity that intersects with the need of a world ignorant of love and solves the absence of justice with compassion. There is no patience in God's reign of love for manipulation. God's choice for worship is a way of life, not just one time acts of piety and ritual. God's way is *shalom* or holistic, transformative well-being.

When the prophet Isaiah proclaimed his word of warning to the nation of Israel, they were in full-blown crisis. Cynicism and apathy had fogged over clarity for the Israelites. The pronouncement of Isaiah 58 came as a harsh wake-up call to God's people. Their attitude had nose dived into navel gazing. They wanted justice for themselves but were unwilling to seek it on behalf of others.

Myopic complaining about the lack of God's response to their worship opened the door for the prophet to speak on God's behalf. The rebellion of God's people was not in their wandering from the constraints of the faith to other religions; rather it was in presuming that ritualistic worship was all God required of God's people. God, through the prophet was accusing the people of some serious things, including using worship to serve their own economic interests. God cannot be manipulated.

The Israelites served themselves under the guise of serving God. They did not understand what it meant to be God's people. God perceives even the appearance of humility as rebellion if God's people ignore injustice and evil. The Israelites did not understand that their mission was to reflect God's nature: a God who related to them in grace compounded by grace. When the Israelites were treated unjustly and cried for deliverance, God heard them and freed them. When they were slaves and exiles, when they were oppressed, God loosed their chains and delivered them from the hands of their enemies. When they were hungry, thirsty, naked, and homeless, God fed, clothed, and sheltered them.

At stake here is the very nature of what it means to be God's people in the world. The prophet's words echo just as strongly to God's church today. God's people have been called to meet the real needs of hunger, pain, injustice, poverty, and oppression. "Is not this the fast I choose: to loose the bonds of injustice, to undo the thongs of the yoke, to let the oppressed go free and to break every yoke? Is it not to share your bread with the hungry, and bring the homeless poor into your house; when you see the naked, to cover them, and not to hid yourself from your own kin?" (Is. 58:6–7). The fasting God chooses is the kind that accompanies advocacy and action on behalf of the voiceless.

While God loves the faithful dearly, God's heartbeat is for all those who are yet to be included in the promise of adoption into God's family. Compassion is not a gift for the few, but for every human being. When Jesus walked the earth, he announced that the kingdom of heaven is here—*now*. This means that God's reign of love that banishes evil and injustice entirely has already arrived and God's people are the activators of love conquering evil.

Mission in Action

Pastor Gary came to a stark realization that Clear Creek Church had stagnated. Somehow the fresh spring of living water that comes from Jesus had come to a standstill at Clear Creek. There was no place for the refreshing water to flow. Because of one compassionate outreach to their neighborhood, members and staff alike realized that God's church is sent to complete God's mission of justice and reconciliation. The people of Clear Creek caught on to the urgency of actively confronting evil and injustice in their city. The congregation realized they gathered in worship in order to be sent in mission.

Early in the process of missional transformation, Clear Creek Church became convinced of the immense value of joining with the ecumenical community to confront injustice. She never wanted to be the heroine in the story for her own sake, but realized she would need the wider body of Christ to join forces in overcoming evil with good. They envisioned the love of God and compassion of Jesus being seen above a congregation's name or identity. Serving compassionately together became the catalyst for reflecting God's image and confronting evil and injustice.

Change at Clear Creek Church began with the dream that perhaps basic health care and social-service networking could be provided at no cost and with no strings attached. The idea never involved reinventing the wheel, especially when resources are already spread thin. Rather, they wanted to harness available services to provide health care services for folks unable to find assistance anywhere else. This became a catalyst for compassionate ministries confronting evil and injustice across the spectrum: poverty, crime, drug abuse, human trafficking. An association of ministers in the Portland area who began praying together in 1993 joined forces to implement the Compassion Connect clinics and support an ongoing not-for-profit clinic in the Portland metropolitan area.

The people of Clear Creek came to a harsh realization of the ways in which evil and injustice infiltrated its community. With courage and tenacity, the congregation sought to confront oppression with the light and hope of God's gospel mission. Now ministries like free health clinics, a not-for-profit wedding dress store, and a design studio for at-risk teenage girls serve to confront evil and injustice. These tenacious people will not allow darkness to overcome the light of God's love.

Adorned in Grace is a beautiful example of this kind of subversive confrontation. It started seemingly by accident. A dress shop owner decided to close. The owner knew secondhand that Gary and his wife Linda personally hosted in their home girls rescued from human trafficking. The storeowner donated 400 dresses to

Linda. Through a series of incredible blessings, Adorned in Grace began to operate as a not-for-profit wedding dress shop. Adorned in Grace provides educational awareness of human trafficking and direct intervention in rescuing girls stuck in the vicious cycle. Additionally, a design studio for youth in at-risk neighborhoods provides skills training and one-on-one mentorship. Under the umbrella of Compassion Connect, Clear Creek Church joins other congregations in the movement to end human slavery.

When God's people confront evil and injustice, beauty and goodness subversively begin to take over. Darkness recedes as the light of God's love confronts evil and injustice. Evil is real, but good is a more potent force. Injustice creeps in, but compassion will win in the end. The people of God must find ways to live into corporate rhythms that allow light to drown out the darkness.

The Crippled Jesus

Bishop Desmond Tutu visited Sant'Egidio Catholic Church in Rome where he saw an old crucifix of Jesus without arms. When he asked about this odd depiction of Christ on the cross, he was told that it reminds the community that God relies on us to do God's work in the world. Bishop Tutu later wrote, "Without us, God has no eyes, without us, God has no ears, without us, God has no arms and hands. God relies on us."[1] In one sense, Jesus is crippled without his body, the church, to accomplish the mission of reconciliation on earth.

Evil and injustice are like storm clouds of darkness on this earth. God's people must act justly so that Isaiah's prophecy may come true, "If you remove the yoke from among you, the pointing of the finger, the speaking of evil, if you offer your food to the hungry and satisfy the needs of the afflicted, then your light shall rise in the darkness and your gloom be like the noonday" (Is. 58:9b–10).

Benediction

May God, who seeks the abolition of every enemy of God's reign of love, give you eyes and ears to recognize injustice and hands and feet to overcome evil with good.
Amen.

Exploration: Confronting Evil and Injustice Together

❧ Pray the collect together.

❧ Imagine watching the girls at the Dress for Freedom event. What emotions do you think you would see? What would prompt the girls to rush to hug the speakers who offered words of hope?

❧ Read Isaiah 58. What is at stake if the people of God do not confront evil and injustice? What has God promised to those who "satisfy the needs of the afflicted"?

❧ Name an evil in your community. What injustice do you see in your neighborhood? How might your missional community take steps to meet these issues head-on?

❧ What type of people can best serve God in the face of evil and injustice? What spiritual practices will form that kind of people?

❧ Speak the benediction as a blessing to one another and as a call to action in God's mission.

Part IV

Holy

The church participates in God's mission by proclaiming to the whole world — all classes and cultures, all ages and genders, all nationalities and races — *that God is holy love and, through Jesus, God is transforming a people who embody that holy love* as empowered and knit together by the Holy Spirit, a sign that the kingdom of God is here.

Ecclesial Practices

Feasting on the Scriptures Together

Receiving the Sacraments Together

Reflecting on God's Character Together

1 Peter 1:13–23; 2:1–3

Therefore prepare your minds for action; discipline yourselves; set all your hope on the grace that Jesus Christ will bring you when he is revealed. Like obedient children, do not be conformed to the desires that you formerly had in ignorance. Instead, as he who called you is holy, be holy yourselves in all your conduct; for it is written, "You shall be holy, for I am holy." If you invoke as Father the one who judges all people impartially according to their deeds, live in reverent fear during the time of your exile. You know that you were ransomed from the futile ways inherited from your ancestors, not with perishable things like silver or gold, but with the precious blood of Christ, like that of a lamb without defect or blemish. He was destined before the foundation of the world, but was revealed at the end of the ages for your sake. Through him you have come to trust in God, who raised him from the dead and gave him glory, so that your faith and hope are set on God. Now that you have purified your souls by your obedience to the truth so that you have genuine mutual love, love one another deeply from the heart. You have been born anew, not of perishable but of imperishable seed, through the living and enduring word of God. . . . Rid yourselves, therefore, of all malice, and all guile, insincerity, envy, and all slander. Like newborn infants, long for the pure, spiritual milk, so that by it you may grow into salvation — if indeed you have tasted that the Lord is good.

Chapter 12

Holy Church

I Peter I:13–23; 2:1–3

TUCKED SAFELY IN THE SATCHELS OF TRUSTED MESSENGERS, THE letter from the respected apostle circulated widely through the outer provinces of Rome. From house church to house church, one tiny gathered band of Christians to the next, the words reached their fearful ears and washed over their tense hearts: *grace and peace be yours in abundance.* This was precisely what they needed to hear. When life around them seemed to decay from corruption, Christians were promised an unfading inheritance.

Life in exile threatened the Christians at every turn. These converts to the Jesus way were young in their faith, still working out what it meant to live as citizens of God's new nation without borders, and far from the center of Christianity's birth. The intangible elements of faith pushed in tension against the dismaying realities around them. The letter's author spoke hope through the fog of their fears, that genuine faith was more precious than gold. The outcome of such faith is salvation. *You have been born anew into a life that will never end, through the enduring Word of God.* The letter must have come as a breath of fresh air to the fledgling Christians. When trials threatened to overwhelm, God's peace broke through and announced that the suffering was only temporary.

The tension increased in the felt discrepancy between the downward mobility of the Jesus way and the demands of the civil authorities for submission to their commands, eventually escalating to emperor worship. Christians scattered throughout Asia Minor were afraid, uncertain, and prone to doubt.

So when the bold instructions from their hero in the faith reached them by courier, it would have spoken volumes. Gathered in the homes of willing hosts for worship and instruction, the faithful listened eagerly to the letters of apostles as they were read aloud. Sponges for the insights of their leaders, the community soaked in the wisdom on the how-to's of their faith. Amidst the ambiguity of exile the converts found handholds for faith in the precious epistle: *Prepare your minds for action. Discipline yourselves. Set all your hope on the grace that Jesus Christ will bring you when he is revealed.*

Instead of conforming to ignorant ways of doing things, the apostle challenged them to set an entirely new pattern for their daily lives: holiness of heart and life. *If current circumstances feel uncertain, be secure by living into the hope of the resurrected Jesus; set your faith on God!*

The epistle called the baby Christians to excellence: *Get rid of all the evil junk! Live on a steady diet of God's nourishing spiritual milk that grows the strong and healthy bones of salvation for lifelong faith.* The readers were reminded that their obedience and purification had already produced genuine mutual love. This was a call to love one another deeply, from the heart.

The circulating letter set the bar high for Christians. Recalling God's words, "You shall be holy, for I am holy," the letter provoked the life of holiness as the way of salvation, even in the unknown territory of exile.

Collect

Holy God,
Whose purity emanates brilliance and glory;
Purify our hearts
So that the beauty of your presence may shine out in
    the darkness;
To you be glory in the church, forever and ever.
Amen.

Habitual Holiness

God's church is holy. The word *holy* means "set apart." God calls the church out of the world's patterns of selfishness and into salvation. God's church is holy in community, that is, an entire people set apart as a means for God's missional end. Holiness does not remove us from the world, but gives us a kind of loving defense so that we might become fully available to the world's brokenness.

Peter addressed his first epistle to faithful Jesus followers dispersed throughout Roman provinces in what is modern day Turkey. As new Christians, theirs was the plight of the resident alien. Their experience of exile was likely two fold: reliving the estrangement of Israel in the wilderness and enduring persecution like Jesus did at the hands of those with political power. The challenge of the letter was to live in obedience to an entirely new way of being. Peter called them to be holy just as God is holy.

Life for Christians in the first century was exilic. Newly baptized followers found themselves a people in the margins, disempowered and homeless. They faced great temptation to return to old patterns of living. Life was unsettled. They had to rely on God for everything. Just as their spiritual ancestors had found it necessary to rely on God's provision in the desert, the current generation had to rely on God for a way forward amidst the threat of trial.

Christians are called to countercultural lives. Everything in God's reign of love is upside down and backwards from the perspective of the unbelieving person. Even in times when Christianity has been the official state religion, the call of holiness is always to downward mobility. Paul described this in graphic detail to the Philippian congregation (Phil. 2:1–8). Jesus' way stands in stark contrast with those in the world who exploit the powerless.

In this precious letter of encouragement, the original readers of 1 Peter received instruction on how to live. *Flee from the old life and rely on the new grace that is yours in God*, their teacher told them. *Be holy in everything you do*, Peter said. *You're already cleansed, so live lives of genuine love.*

Like bright-eyed toddlers daring to walk into the world, these brand new believers had fresh ears for the life of faith. God's love was described as spiritual milk. The apostle admonished the young Christians to crave nourishment that can only be found in God so that they might grow strong in the life of salvation. The implication here is not that milk is inferior to solid foods, as elsewhere in the New Testament, but rather that this deeply nourishing milk of God's Word is both gift and grace.

This milk is a foretaste of fuller salvation yet to come. Craving pure spiritual milk will grow baby Christians into maturity just like a mother's milk nurtures newborns toward healthy lives.

This passage calls newly born babes in the faith to become who they were created to be. New people doing new things, living new lives. In today's vernacular, the imagery of verse 13 might be translated as "roll up your sleeves and get to work." The apostle challenges the new believers to live into their calling as royal priests, a holy nation, as God's own people. "Once you were not a people, but now you are God's people; once you had not received mercy, but now you have received mercy" (1 Pet. 2:9–10). Even as resident aliens in a foreign land, the apostle believed that holiness would be the credible witness of God's people to their surrounding neighbors.

According to the Nicene Creed, a premier mark of God's church is that the church is holy. The universal sent-ness of God's people on a mission finds expression in the holiness of God's church. The credibility of the church's witness depends on it. Holiness is apostolic in nature. Holiness equips the church to practice its vocation as ambassadors of love and grace. Holiness is the evidence of being saved. God's church is sent in universal unity to live as witness to God's worldwide reconciliation of all things and all people.

Holiness in Motion

God's church is formed in holiness as it practices feasting on the Scriptures together (see chapter 13). The Scriptures are the ultimate letter of instruction from God through the collective voices of the prophets, leaders, poets, song-leaders, apostles, disciples, and witnesses. They tell the story of history's main character, God, and the purity of love that resonates from the core of God's nature. In reflecting deeply on God's story and mission of reconciliation through the narrative of the Scriptures, God's church will be magnetized to the life of holiness.

When God's church practices receiving the sacraments together (see chapter 14), the church is formed in holiness by a sacred means of grace. The sacramental acts of baptism and Eucharist increase capacity for holiness in the life of both individual believers and the community of saints. Dramatizing the entrance of the believer into the life, death, and resurrection of Christ, baptism initiates and demonstrates a holy life that has been cleansed of sin. Nourishing our lives with the spiritual food of Christ when celebrating the Eucharist empowers holy living. Practicing these sacraments together, God's church is made holy at the intersection of our cooperation.

By practicing reflecting on God's character together (see chapter 15), God's church is formed into the imago Dei. When God's people practice reflecting on who God is, what God wills, and how God loves, holiness follows. Holiness does not just happen but is continually fanned into flame when God's people choose to live into the image in which they have been created. Thinking deeply on who God is and how we are to participate in God's mission is sure to invite holiness to put down deep roots and grow up a strong community of faith.

A Lighthouse Called Holiness

When we read the New Testament through a missional lens, we ask the "how" questions. How shall we witness? How shall we be salt, light, and yeast? How shall the life of Jesus be manifested in our bodies? These are the questions that lead the church to live worthy of its calling (Eph. 4:1). The vocation of the church is to live a holy life, equipped by the Spirit, as it is sent to help accomplish God's mission of reconciliation. Holiness is not so much about the absence of brokenness as it is the presence of love to overcome evil with good.

*The church participates in God's mission by proclaiming
to the whole world — all classes and cultures, all ages
and genders, all nationalities and races — that God is
holy love and, through Jesus, God is transforming a
people who embody that holy love as empowered and knit
together by the Holy Spirit, a sign that the kingdom of
God is here.*

God's church is marked by holy love because *God is holy love.*
Further, *through Jesus, God is transforming a people who embody that
holy love.* Holiness is the beacon of God's love to a world desperate
for reconciliation. Just like the Gospel witness put it, "A city on a
hill cannot be hidden" (Matt. 5:14).

Benediction

*May the holy God make you holy through and through
so that you will brightly shine in the shadows of sin
and bring the warmth of God's love to the chill of evil.
Amen.*

Exploration: Holy Church

❧ Pray the collect together.

❧ Imagine receiving threats because you are a Christian, then receiving the letter of encouragement from Peter. What emotions might the church experience in that situation? What gives you courage to live faithfully as Christians?

❧ Read 1 Peter 1:13–16. What gifts come from God? What is an appropriate response to God's gifts?

❧ Read 1 Peter 1:22. How does soul purity impact the church? Read 1 Peter 2:1. How might ridding the church of these qualities affect the church's witness?

❧ Why would those who crafted the Nicene Creed consider holiness as one of the four most important characteristics of the church?

❧ Describe a clear demonstration of God's holiness in the world. How can your missional community show your neighborhood the purity of God's love?

❧ Speak the benediction as a blessing to one another and as a call to action in God's mission.

Chapter 13

A Grand Narrative

Feasting on the Scriptures Together

S ANDI AND BART PULLED INTO THE PARKING LOT OF THEIR FAVORITE bagel shop for lunch. As they walked from their car, they noticed a man in dirty clothes standing on the corner holding a sign. *Was he here before or are we just now noticing him?* That morning their pastor had preached on compassion. The call to serve was still ringing in their ears.

Instead of simply giving money, Sandi and Bart felt prompted to ask the man if he would like to eat with them. He asked if his wife could join them. Sandi and Bart looked across the parking lot to where a woman held a sign too.

As the four shared their lives over bagels, Sandi and Bart learned that Liz and Duane had both lost jobs and were living in a tent city with about thirty other people in a forested area not far from their home. Sandi and Bart realized that, as in the book of Acts, God had appointed this meeting for God's purposes. This experience led Sandi and Bart to begin a ministry to the people in the tent community, regularly bringing food, clothing, and tarps to those who lacked the basic necessities of life.

A few months before, a personal encounter with a weary homeless woman at his local library had sparked Pastor Brad of Hillside Church to begin a search of the Bible to discover God's heart for the poor and hurting. As the Scripture's call to serve came alive in

Brad, he knew he had to share it with his congregation. Brad and the leadership team committed to place God's story at the center of the congregation's life.

Over the next several years they challenged the congregation to immerse itself in the reading of the Bible. As a congregation they took several "read together" journeys, often connecting the readings with their pastor's preaching and teaching. One series took the congregation on a fifty-two week, chronological excursion from Genesis to Revelation. Another series revealed the biblical mandate to seek justice and care for the least of these by exploring passages from the Law, the Prophets, and the teachings of Christ in the Gospels.

Stories, like Sandi and Bart's, multiplied. Each time the congregation plunged itself anew into the biblical narrative, God's Spirit brought a fresh stirring to the hearts and minds of the people. These stirrings led to new levels of engagement in God's mission, catapulting the congregation into their community in creative ways. The congregation began to see the world and their own neighborhood through the lens of God's missional word.

Since those initial awakenings, Hillside Church has celebrated as individuals have come to faith in Jesus Christ. New people have been embraced into the ongoing life of their congregation. The congregation now engages in volunteer-driven initiatives such as advocacy for the shelterless, food and clothing distribution, addiction treatment, and foster parenting programs. As Hillside Church has pursued opportunities to feast on the Scriptures together, they have been energized to live out God's call to be the church in their city.

Collect

Ever-speaking God,
Whose voice echoes through the great story of the
Bible;
May we hunger and thirst for your word,
So that as you speak, we may be nourished for the life
of faith;

*We ask this through Jesus Christ, the eternal and
living Word, who lives and reigns with you and the
Holy Spirit.*
Amen.

A Story-Formed People

At the heart of the Christian faith is a story. Employing a variety of styles and authors and spanning generations, the Bible tells the sweeping saga of God's mission: creation, incarnation, and re-creation. Rooted in history yet teeming with imagination, the Scriptures do more than provide a list of laws to be followed. They present a divine drama whose primary character is a loving God and whose purpose is to draw us in as key players. The call to remember and be shaped by the story of God reverberates throughout the biblical narrative.

The Israelites sought to stay faithful in the present by remembering God's redemptive work in the past. They did so by rehearsing God's salvation story with their children both in the home and in community worship. "When your children ask you in time to come, 'What is the meaning of the decrees and the statutes and the ordinances that the Lord our God has commanded you?' then you shall say to your children, 'We were Pharaoh's slaves in Egypt, but the Lord brought us out of Egypt with a mighty hand'" (Deut. 6:20–21).

Remembering is also a centerpiece of the Passover celebration. "You shall observe the festival of unleavened bread, for on this very day I brought your companies out of the land of Egypt: you shall observe this day throughout your generations as a perpetual ordinance" (Ex. 12:17).

Jesus' life and ministry was immersed in Scripture. He would have known the story from an early age and his experience of the Scriptures in the home, synagogue, and temple would have deeply shaped his worldview. According to the Gospels, Jesus conceived of his own ministry within the larger context of Israel's history. When

Jesus was tempted in the wilderness, he quoted Scripture (Matt. 4; Luke 4). When he spoke in the synagogue, he identified himself as fulfilling biblical prophecy (Luke 4:21). At the Last Supper, Jesus recalled the Passover story and reframed it in terms of his own death: "This is my body given for you; do this in remembrance of me" (Luke 22:19). When Jesus suffered on the cross, he cried out a prayer from Psalm 22.

Following the basic structure of synagogue worship, the reading and hearing of the Scriptures was a centerpiece of the gatherings of Jesus' earliest followers. The Psalms served as the church's original hymnal. The Old Testament canon continued to serve as the backdrop of God's unfolding story through this new covenant community. The written word, read in the midst of the congregation, was understood to be the life-giving Word of God breathing into them and energizing them for mission.

The post-Pentecost church also gathered together and "devoted themselves to the apostles' teaching" (Acts 2:42). Eventually written down and officially adopted as Scripture, the apostles' teaching served as an authoritative voice for the church, shaping and articulating Christianity's developing doctrines and serving as a record of God's activity. Hearing and responding to the teaching of those who walked with Jesus was intrinsically linked to the life and mission of the community.

The church, translating and interpreting the Scriptures anew in each generation, has continued to confess that God is revealed through the ancient message of the text. When the power and presence of the Holy Spirit is joined with faithful engagement of the Bible, each encounter with Holy Scripture becomes a life-changing encounter with God.

A Story-starved People

If we believe God speaks by the Holy Spirit through the Scriptures, it stands to reason the Bible will hold a central place in the church's life. While this is true for many communities, it is not the case for some, especially in the evangelical stream. Interestingly, much of the dissatisfaction about the absence of God's word comes from the pews, not from evangelical preachers.

People lament the exchange of solid biblical and theological teaching that immerses participants in the story of God for moralistic self-help or how-to talks and seminars with little scriptural basis. In these situations the gospel is truncated to a few bullet points that help people become better parents, lovers, employees, citizens, and churchgoers. These readings offer little more than nuggets of wisdom to apply to life. Many are starving for teaching and storytelling that brings us face to face with the gospel and leads beyond application to transformation.

Returning the reading and interpretation of Scripture as a central act in gatherings of worship can be a powerful means for the church to corporately interact with the word of God on a regular basis. While there is value in topical preaching and teaching, there is a greater need for the people to be exposed to full units of thought and the sweep of biblical narrative. For extended passages, it is possible to employ drama, reader's theater, or the creative use of video. Using a variety of trained readers from the community helps the church see that this word is to be embodied by all, not just a few.

A congregation can experience the power of God's word when the themes of the Scriptures shape the worship service itself. Following the Christian calendar and employing the lectionary or other cycles of Scripture readings help connect a congregation with the church in other parts of the world.

The Psalms provide rich resources for corporate prayers and songs of lament, thanksgiving, praise, and supplication. The various genres of Scripture offer a rich and beautiful tapestry for interpreters, teachers, preachers, poets, and artists to create environments designed to lead us into an encounter with God.

Bible reading plans can be employed as a means for a missional community to walk through the story of God together. Technology and social media, including websites and mobile Bible apps, have opened wide the door for communities to grapple and interact with texts and their meanings — anytime, anywhere. This provides instant connection between the message of the ancient text and the challenges of mission in daily life.

Fresh winds are blowing. Many yearn to understand and study the Bible in context and desire to grapple with its meaning within the believing community. There is a longing to recover the Bible as an overarching story that invites not just intellectual understanding but deep participation. Missional communities that make the Scriptures central to their life realize that study of the Bible is not an end in itself. Instead, the church is called to feast on the Scriptures in order to nourish it for a life of mission.

Extending God's Story

Every Sunday at five in the morning, a team of people from Hillside Church head out to the bridges in Petaluma to bring hot coffee and sandwiches to the people living there. As the team converses and shares food with those without shelter, they discover a spiritual hunger. Each week there are multiple requests for prayer. As a result of this ministry, several individuals have discovered the relentless love of Christ and a spiritual home at Hillside Church. The feast of Scripture this congregation has experienced has led and empowered them to feed others, both physically and spiritually.

The Bible is more than something the church just uses or applies. It presents a grand narrative of God's missional activity in which all are invited to join. The Bible's message is not just to be understood but embraced and lived out in the power of the Holy Spirit for the sake of the world.

Benediction

May God, who has spoken and continues speaking,
form you through the word of the Lord planted deep in
your heart so that your life in Christ tells God's story
of love.
Amen.

Exploration: Feasting on the Scriptures Together

❧ Pray the collect together.

❧ Sandi and Bart ate with Liz and Duane at the bagel shop. In what ways were their actions more than the sharing of food? How do you suppose Liz and Duane felt when they received more than a meal?

❧ Read 2 Timothy 3:16–17. What does it mean to call Scripture "God-breathed"? According to these verses, what is the ultimate purpose of Scripture?

❧ Reflect on the weekly rhythm of your missional community. Describe how the community engages the Scriptures. What might strengthen your community as you seek to "let the word of Christ dwell in you richly" (Col. 3:16)?

❧ Think about the teachers and artists in your missional community who help the Scriptures come alive. Speak words of affirmation to these persons.

❧ Speak the benediction as a blessing to one another and as a call to action in God's mission.

Chapter 14

Embodied Grace

Receiving the Sacraments Together

ONE BITTERLY COLD EASTER SUNDAY, PASTOR DEBORAH STEPPED out of her car and into the morning air. Instead of walking into a building, however, she went to a fountain located on the corner of Boston Common, one of the oldest city parks in the United States. She had put on several layers of clothing to keep warm as she prepared to lead worship.

A small group assembled as Deborah took her place behind a makeshift altar constructed from a rolling cart she had borrowed from a congregation across the street. As the wind whipped through the trees above, the sounds of worship could be heard in the park below.

Sixteen unhoused people sat on the concrete park benches near the altar, lifting their voices to God in praise and prayer. After a brief devotional on the Scripture reading, Pastor Deborah invited the people to share. Songs, cries of lament, and stories of hope and despair from life on the streets emerged from the group.

Pastor Deborah raised her hands above her head, lifting a plate of bread and a chalice of wine. She looked into the weary eyes of the people gathered, most of whom had not received the sacrament in years. She spoke the familiar words, "The body of Christ given for you; the blood of Christ shed for you." As the service drew to a close, people gathered around as Deborah shared peanut butter and jelly sandwiches with members of her newly formed parish.

Earlier that morning, she had been filled with apprehension, unsure if anyone would even come. But in the week following, people who had not even attended came up to her on the street to tell her they could not wait to see her the next Sunday. Word traveled fast. By the third week, the people told her they needed a name for *their* congregation. "This is Common Cathedral," one man had said. The name stuck.

Pastor Deborah had been meeting with people on the street for some time, listening to their stories and befriending them. She often walked through the parks and subways sharing sandwiches with the hungry. As she got to know the people, she encountered loneliness, hopelessness, and isolation. In this bleak environment Pastor Deborah felt compelled to celebrate Communion.

The Lord's Table has become the centerpiece not only of Common Cathedral's worship but also of the community's life together. Pastor Deborah makes use of the traditional Anglican liturgy, adapting the style to fit her context. As the congregation has grown, it has become more diverse.

Housed congregations have become involved, often coming to Boston Common on Sundays to worship. Those who are able bring food to share with those who are hungry. As urban homeless persons gather next to employed suburban dwellers, one thing brings them together: their desperate need for God's grace and the embrace of God's people.

What started as a simple celebration of the Lord's Supper has become a vibrant missional community that now celebrates the Eucharist every Sunday at Boston Common, rain or shine. The ministry provides midweek programs to bring people together and engage the needs of their neighborhood. For Common Cathedral, the Eucharist has become more than a symbol. It is a way of life.

Collect

Holy God,
Who makes your presence known in water, bread, and
*   wine;*
Take our ordinary, everyday lives and make them
*   extraordinary by the presence of your Spirit*
So that the grace of Christ may be shared through us;
We pray in the all-sufficient name of Jesus.
Amen.

Spirit-infused, Common Elements

The sacraments have been a subject of debate throughout the history of the church. Arguments, divisions, and wars have been fueled by disagreements over their meaning and role in the church's life. And yet they play a central part in the worship and faith of a majority of the world's believers. Christians have always believed that God uses the physical, the common, and the ordinary to communicate grace and love to God's people.

Scripture declares that "God saw everything that he had made, and indeed, it was very good" (Gen. 1:31) and that "the heavens are telling the glory of God; and the firmament proclaims his handiwork" (Ps. 19:1). Sacramental practice is grounded in the scriptural confession that God's good world, though fallen, is redeemable. Furthermore, it boldly proclaims that redeemed creation actually becomes a means of grace, pointing the world to its Creator.

Throughout Scripture, sign-acts and physical objects served as a means for people to communicate with God. God delivered God's people through water. Israel was led through the wilderness by a cloud and pillar of fire. Physical objects were used in Israel's worship and later in Christian worship to enable people to express devotion and experience God's presence. Scripture even calls human beings themselves to be a means of blessing to the world (Gen. 12:3).

Christians believe and teach that God redeems fallen creation from the inside out. In the incarnation, "the Word became flesh and lived among us" (John 1:14). God took on the physical stuff of earth and literally embodied grace, redeeming humankind. Jesus was a *living* sacrament.

The church, redeemed by grace, now serves as the physical expression of God's presence in the world. As a faithful sign points to that which it signifies, the church points not to itself but to the splendor and majesty of God, thus fulfilling its missional call in the world.

In the sacraments, God's love is made visible in the midst of the community as the church enacts the story of God. Baptism forms and signifies our identity as Christ's own and our initiation into God's church. From the waters, we are sent on mission. The Eucharist nourishes us for a communal life in Christ marked by thanksgiving and service. To call these *means of grace* implies that they are not primarily *our* work, although we have a part to play. Sacraments remind us that life comes from a source outside ourselves as a gift to be received.

Attempts to explain and categorize the sacraments can be helpful. However, it is ultimately the practice of the sacraments within the context of a believing community that brings missional vitality, particularly when it is understood that the grace given to us is forming us to be a blessing to the world.

God uses common and ordinary things such as water, bread, and wine to communicate God's grace and to form our identity as God's people. As the church participates in God's grace, it is made holy and set apart for God's mission. By the work of the Spirit, the church becomes, like its Lord, a grace-filled sacrament to be given to the world.

Identification as Christ's Body

On the day of Pentecost, the Spirit-filled Peter preached to the crowds in Jerusalem and many responded by believing the gospel. Following Peter's sermon, Luke provided a snapshot of the early church's life together. "So those who welcomed his message were baptized, and that day about three thousand persons were added. They devoted themselves to the apostles' teaching and fellowship, to the breaking of bread and the prayers" (Acts 2:41–42).

Luke revealed that the most pivotal moment in the missional development of the church (Pentecost) was marked by sacramental celebration. He also pointed to the role of the sacraments as central elements in the process of conversion and growth in the Christian life. The pattern is laid out: baptism as a mark of entry into the community followed by engagement in its life, including the regular practice of breaking bread.

Of course, terminology has changed since Acts and there is a wide variety of practice among Christians today. The church has had centuries to reflect and debate on what is actually happening in the sacraments. Nevertheless, Luke called the church back to a common life that is marked by rich and frequent sacramental celebrations as a means of experiencing and bearing witness to God's gracious activity among his people.

Many communities have gone to one of two extremes when it comes to the sacraments, influenced in part by their theological tradition. Some have taken them for granted and risk losing their meaning and purpose. For these communities, sacraments can become rote, lifeless rituals. Others have completely neglected the sacraments. In an attempt to make them "special," inconsistent celebration or unclear teaching has actually communicated that they are unimportant.

Mission suffers in both instances. Effective missional communities work hard to maintain consistent, purposeful practice while recognizing the role of sacraments as signs that point to Christ and edify the body of Christ.

Many communities are recovering the important role baptism plays in conversion as an initiating and identity-forming act. As a means of reminding people of this truth, some missional communities place a water-filled baptismal font in their worship space each week, whether there is a baptism being celebrated or not. When a baptism is being celebrated, the whole congregation gathers around to witness and participate. This visible symbol reminds the community every time it gathers that it is called to a new life of mission in the pattern of Jesus himself.

Missional communities understand that sacraments are shared acts, not just something that a priest or pastor does for an individual. Communion is being recovered as a common meal, which draws the community together to encounter the risen Christ and to be nourished for a life of mission. Many are rediscovering the early church's pattern of weekly table celebrations. Often these are connected to or followed by a community meal.

Thought should be given to how the sacraments are celebrated and what implications exist for mission. In the North American context that tends to focus on the individual, the need for sacraments to emphasize the life of the whole community is greater than ever. With careful reflection and intentional practice, sacraments can become powerful grace-filled encounters with God that propel the church out to mission in the world.

Celebration

Common Cathedral shows what kind of community a rich, Spirit-filled sacramental life will produce. What began as a simple act of worship in a small gathering has become a weekly rhythm for a growing congregation. Each time someone from the community is released from prison or celebrates a year of sobriety, it is celebrated at the Lord's Table. Each time a small victory is won in a support group meeting or an insight is gained in Bible study, praise rises at the Eucharist. When someone who is hungry receives food, it is an extension of the Communion meal.

The sacraments are not merely a witness of our spiritual journey, though they include that. They are, by the power and presence of the Holy Spirit, significant means of grace through which God forms the life of God's church for the sake of God's mission in the world. As missional communities gratefully receive the grace of God in the sacraments, they are empowered to give it away.

Benediction

May God, who created water and fruit and grain,
use the common elements of life to reveal God's
marvelous grace so that all who encounter you also
encounter Christ.
Amen.

Exploration: Receiving the Sacraments Together

❧ Pray the collect together.

❧ Put yourself in the place of a displaced person who often feels isolated, even from the church. Describe what your response might be if the church came to you in a city park.

❧ Describe an experience of baptism or Communion that made a deep impression on your life. What made the experience so significant to you?

❧ There are three components of every sacrament: scriptural words of institution, the material elements used to make the sign, and the physical action required. Read 1 Corinthians 11:23–26. Identify these three components for Communion. Identify these components for baptism.

❧ The sacraments can be rich and meaningful experiences of God's grace in drawing God's people together and inspiring mission. Brainstorm some ways you might strengthen your sacramental celebrations so as to realize those outcomes.

❧ Speak the benediction as a blessing to one another and as a call to action in God's mission.

Chapter 15

Finding God in the Ordinary

Reflecting on God's Character Together

FIVE MEMBERS OF THE HEALING CHOIR FROM BETHEL CHURCH STEPPED into the living room of the guesthouse. They greeted Barbara. Too weak to stand, Barbara welcomed her visitors from where she lay covered by a blanket on the sofa.

Barbara and her husband traveled to Boston to consult with doctors at Brigham and Women's Hospital. Late-stage lung cancer, the doctors suspected at the time. The healing choir listened carefully as Barbara spoke, but only with one ear. They also listened for God's guidance so they could pray with power.

Then the visitors began to sing. The sound of hymns filled that living room. A divine-tuned hearing detected heavenly voices as it seemed like the angels joined in. God's grace settled on all as words, melody, and harmony formed the strands of a lifeline: "a threefold cord is not quickly broken" (Eccl. 4:12). Barbara requested that they sing a hymn that had great meaning for her, and then a second favorite. She felt her spirit quickened as her visitors sang.

Sean, the leader of the choir, reached into his pocket for a vial of oil; then he knelt beside Barbara. With his finger tracing the shape of the cross, Sean anointed Barbara's forehead with the oil of gladness, not mourning. They prayed fervently for God's healing touch.

When the healing choir left that house, the Holy Spirit remained with Barbara. Love. Joy. Peace.

A few years ago, the pastor of Bethel Church had a growing awareness of the profound need in people's lives for God's healing touch. Now at the end of each month during a Sunday worship service, a member of the pastoral staff leads the anointing and prayers for all who call on the church for help. Bethel Church has become a means of grace for many people.

The healing choir goes to those who cannot come to a Sunday service. Through the healing choir, the grace of God evident when Bethel Church gathers on Sundays extends to places and persons who intensely need God's peace. More than fifteen people have joined the choir, but never more than four or five go as representatives of Bethel Church to sing and pray with the sick person.

Once a month the healing choir gathers for a time of fellowship, singing, and prayer. This gathering equips and nourishes them for the ministry they share. Laughter punctuates the mealtime. Then they take the hymnal to sing.

> *Does Jesus care when my heart is pained*
> *Too deeply for mirth and song,*
> *As the burdens press, and the cares distress,*
> *And the way grows weary and long?*

Members of the healing choir recognize their own need for God's healing touch. They have joined the choir not because of their great musical ability, but because they recognize the power of music as a means of grace.

> *O yes, He cares; I know He cares!*
> *His heart is touched with my grief.*
> ~ Frank Graeff (1901)

They stop singing to talk with each other about how they see God at work in their lives. Their vision and conversation expands to consider God's activity in the whole world. As they pray together, they quietly rest in the loving care of God.

When the healing choir sang for Barbara, she said, "If I die, I'll be okay because I'll get to be with Jesus. If I live, I get to finish

Marks of the Missional Church

my quilt." Several months later Barbara sent them a photo of the completed quilt.

Collect

Jesus, our Prince of Peace,
You wept with Mary and Martha outside their
    brother's tomb;
Cause light and life to triumph over darkness and
    death
So that the glory of God may radiate to the whole
    world
And praise may reverberate throughout the heavens.
Amen.

Insights from Theological Reflection

One day Jesus and the disciples walked past a man blind from birth. In the midst of their journey, the disciples asked Jesus a question: "Rabbi, who sinned, this man or his parents, that he was born blind?" (John 9:2). Their question asked for a theological explanation of the man's condition. Right in the middle of a stroll the disciples wanted to talk about holiness and sin. Can the physical condition of blindness be explained in the language of theology?

This story illustrates what educational theorists call the action-reflection model of learning. In this story, Jesus and the disciples encounter the blind man (*action*). The disciples asked Jesus a question and Jesus responded (*reflection*).

The disciples presented Jesus with two options: *Who sinned, the man or his parents? A or B?* Jesus replied, *C*, then stooped to mix saliva with dirt to make an emollient that he placed on the blind man's eyes. "Go, wash in the pool of Siloam," Jesus instructed the man. So the man "went and washed and came back able to see" (John 9:7).

When the Pharisees saw the formerly blind man, they did some theological reflection of their own. They started with their understanding of the Law, the result of previous reflection, not the action of the healing of a blind man. Their logic went something like this: godly persons obey the Mosaic Law; Mosaic Law forbids work on the Sabbath; Jesus worked/healed on the Sabbath; Jesus is not a godly person.

Some people argued with this conclusion and insisted that an ungodly person could not perform such a marvelous sign. The Pharisees, however, had no room in their thinking to consider anything other than a conclusion that started with their understanding of the Mosaic Law, not the work of God evident in the healed man.

The Pharisees called on the man's parents to confirm he had been born blind. The parents recounted the facts, but since they worried that they might be "put out of the synagogue," they disengaged from the theological reflection. "He is of age; ask him," they said (John 9:22, 23).

The logic of the blind man began with the startling fact that he could see: only God can make a blind man see; God uses godly persons for miraculous signs; God used Jesus; Jesus is a godly person. Action-reflection: the man acknowledged that something marvelous had occurred and through a reflective process gave credit to God.

We find this type of reflective process in various places in the Bible. David looked into the night sky and his theological reflection caused him to exclaim, "O Lord, our Sovereign, how majestic is your name in all the earth!" (Ps. 8:9). After the shepherds visited the baby Jesus, Luke said that Mary "pondered" all that had occurred. The Greek word used here means "to put together" as in to make connections or meaning. Mary reflected on what she had experienced and in doing so stitched things together so as to reveal the tapestry of God's redemptive actions. Paul urgently begged God for deliverance from a thorn in the flesh, but through theological reflection he saw God's grace at work in his weakness. These people considered their experiences and through theological reflection recognized the movement of God.

A Reflective Spiral

A missional community follows a similar process as it reflects on God's involvement in the world. Since the missional community eagerly seeks to join in God's mission already begun, it attempts to discern how God is at work. This sensitivity to divine action does not come from the flip of a switch, but when the community slows down to pay attention to the nuances of life. It emerges when companions listen to each other's insights and seeks to make connections of various ideas.

Seeking to understand God's work requires continuous reflection since every morning God's mercy shines ever brighter. The rhythm of living together as a missional community, the sharing of life experiences, naturally flows into conversations and reflections on how God is evident in those experiences. Just as this occurred *on the way* for the disciples in John 9, so this rhythm arises organically in the life of a missional community.

Three questions can guide the reflection process. First, *What is the sign?* This step in the process involves noticing the human aspects of life and relationships. Some spiritual practices, such as the Ignatian communal examen, stress the importance of attention to emotions at this point. A strong emotional response may help a missional community identify an area that warrants watchful consideration and fervent listening.

Second, *What does the sign signify?* This question leads the missional community toward a theological understanding of the sign. Prior study of Scripture, theology, and Christian tradition contribute to the reflection at this point. After Jesus used a whip to drive out those who had turned the temple into a livestock sale barn, the disciples "remembered that it was written, 'Zeal for your house will consume me'" (John 2:17). The disciples' reflection on the action they witnessed included making the connection with David and Psalm 69. A missional community will ponder its experience by making connections with orthodox Christianity as it seeks to find meaning in the experience.

Third, *What is the significance for life?* Theological reflection always moves toward a practical embodiment of the faith. Looking intently at the *sign* and the *signified* will uncover the *significance*. An experience will point to God that has ramifications which shape a community's embodiment of the gospel in the future.

The action-reflection process is more than a loop that repeats *ad infinitum*. A better term to describe this rhythm is a reflective spiral. As a missional community integrates new experiences with previous insights, the reflective spiral pulls the missional community deeper into "The love of Christ that surpasses knowledge, so that [they] may be filled with all the fullness of God" (Eph. 3:19). This process helps a missional community understand God more fully and themselves in relation to God, thus, they can better participate in God's mission to reconcile the world under God's reign. By paying careful attention to its practices and actions, a missional community grows in its understanding of God and itself as the body of Christ. The ecclesial practice of theological reflection involves focused integrative thought for learning, insights, and meaning making.

Missional Action, Inquisitive Reflection

The evangelical church has been through a period that utilized the traditional school model for Christian education. One or two teachers work with students using curriculum designed for that age group. The education committee in this type of congregation seeks to make the Sunday school classroom similar to what children have during the week at a public school. Teens and adults have their own curriculum too. The desire and goal, often unstated, is for students to take what they learn on Sundays and incorporate it in their lives during the week. Unfortunately, learning in this manner rarely leads to increased missional engagement for the sake of the world.

We propose another way. We urge a missional community to begin finding ways to embody the gospel in its neighborhood. As the community engages in missional life, they pay attention to the signs of God's activity among them. They intentionally set time to talk to each other about what the signs signify. They let their growing understanding of God and their role in God's mission to reshape their next activity as a missional community. And all will rejoice as marks of God's kingdom becomes evident to all.

Benediction

May the ever-present God make you aware of divine grace at work in the world so that you offer yourselves as a means of grace to further God's reconciling action toward all.
Amen.

Exploration: Reflecting on God Together

✎ Pray the collect together.

✎ The visit from the healing choir brought comfort and strength to Barbara. Describe a time when a group of friends helped you remember the goodness of God. Tell about a hymn or song that gives you courage.

✎ Read John 9:24–34. The Pharisees started their theological reflection with their understanding of Mosaic Law while the formerly blind man started his theological reflection with his experience of God's miraculous touch. Explore how these two starting places set the trajectory for the two conclusions.

✎ The disciples asked a question, then presented Jesus with two possible answers. Instead of A or B, Jesus chose C (John 9:2–3). How might your missional community be sensitive to God's work that may be beyond all options previously considered?

✎ Describe a time when something happened to you and after reflection on that experience you began to see God at work.

✎ Describe a time when because of the reflection spiral your missional community became more effective in proclaiming and embodying the gospel.

✎ Speak the benediction as a blessing to one another and as a call to action in God's mission.

Part V

One

The church participates in God's mission by proclaiming to the whole world — all classes and cultures, all ages and genders, all nationalities and races — that God is holy love and, through Jesus, God is transforming a people who embody that holy love *as empowered and knit together by the Holy Spirit, a sign that the kingdom of God is here.*

Ecclesial Practices

Building Community Together

Serving Compassionately Together

Worshiping Together

Ephesians 4:1–6

I therefore, the prisoner in the Lord, beg you to lead a life worthy of the calling to which you have been called, with all humility and gentleness, with patience, bearing with one another in love, making every effort to maintain the unity of the Spirit in the bond of peace. There is one body and one Spirit, just as you were called to the one hope of your calling, one Lord, one faith, one baptism, one God and Father of all, who is above all and through all and in all.

Chapter 16

One Church

Ephesians 4:1–6

L ETTERS DELIVERED FROM JAIL ARE WORTH A READ. FROM INSIDE
prison, things that matter suddenly come into sharper focus.
If a letter from captivity is being delivered to you, it might
be time to clean the wax from your ears and listen up.

When the words etched on parchment from inside those dank
Roman prison walls reached the ears of the faithful gathered in
freedom beyond, the congregation in Ephesus must have clung to
the apostle's letter. He spared no passion in appealing to the community to live in unity. He practically begged them to lead lives
worthy of their calling. After all, God was calling.

What if, suggested the apostle to the church outside the prison
walls, *what if you were chained together by peace instead of being divided
by petty differences? Just think of what a witness it will be to the watching world if peace binds you together. What if humility, gentleness, and
patience mark your life together in community, even as you make room
for flaws and quirks that are an inevitable part of humans attempting to
live life together?*

The apostle knew his audience. They were Jews and Gentiles,
now unified under Christ's banner, learning to live into the tricky
business of communal life and faith. Just a few decades before this
plea from prison, these folks had been sworn enemies and entirely
exclusive of each other.

The apostle understood well that unity does not mean uniformity. That is why he seemed to place emphasis on unity instead of the need to convince the other to believe precisely the same thing. The apostle encouraged the budding Christian community to live in such a way that unity would be their primary witness to the world. Pursuing their common call, to live lives of love on the reconciliation mission, would make them one. The apostle knew that to make the invisible transformation of God visible to one another and the watching world, unity was absolutely necessary. Hence the urgency in begging them to live lives worthy of their calling.

To the apostle stuck in that prison, the calling of God was loud and clear. He was not about to waste away in despair. Deep beneath the ground, shuttered from the light of day, the limitless presence and power of Christ was all the more real. God's love was not limited to sacred places only. Faith suddenly seemed bright now, more real, and more compassionate in his sufferings. He desperately wanted the faith community on the outside to inhale a fresh breath of the Spirit, to see the true freedom of God's love reflected in the unity of Christ's body. Oh how he longed for the sheep he had shepherded to truly grasp the magnificence of God's love manifest in the unity of God's people. Would they listen? Would they hear his impassioned pleas from prison?

Collect

> *God of unity in diversity,*
> *Who has revealed yourself as God in three persons;*
> *Make us one as you are One*
> *So that the world will believe in Jesus as Savior and*
> *   Lord;*
> *All praise to the Triune God, who is over all and in all*
> *   and through all.*
> *Amen.*

Chains of Peace

God's church is one. The church has been called to one hope because there is one Lord, one faith, one baptism, one God who is over all and in all and through all. God's church is sent universally to be holy as God is holy so that its witness before a watching world is unified. The church is apostolic, catholic, holy, and, therefore, *one*.

Seems impossible, does it not? A person need only listen to the chitchat in a local coffee shop for mere moments before differences of opinion bubble to the surface between friends or strangers. Observing a city council meeting or listening to the debate on the floor of the United Nations provides evidence that differences between humans make themselves known simply by more than one showing up to the discussion. And that's before we look to the church. According to a 2011 study by the Pew Forum on Religious and Public life, there are approximately 41,000 Christian denominations encompassing about 2 billion Christians worldwide.[1] If Internet traffic is any indication, there seems to be as many varieties of belief as there are people.

Is the oneness of God's church possible? God initiated the church in that way. Unity is found in common love and worship of one God who permeates every inch of creation with love, not in uniformity. When the apostle wrote to the congregation in Ephesus, a letter likely circulated widely throughout the congregations in Asia Minor, he strongly urges them to live in alignment with their identity as lovers of one God in one faith through one baptism.

The idea that the entire human family can be unified is unique to the Christian mission. The Ephesian epistle painted a picture of cosmic unity and redemption of all things. Chapter 4 represents a shift from the apostle inviting his audience to *remember* who they are *in Christ*, to begging his readers to *persevere in living* as new creations *in Christ*.

The foundation of all Christian virtue is found in the apostle's admonition to *bear with one another in love*. This has far-reaching communal implications. Three virtues sum up the holy life of the community: humility, gentleness, and patience. These three allow Christ followers to live together and to support and sustain each other in love. The apostle shows in this epistle that maintaining the unity of the Spirit in the chains of peace is the kind of effort that grows out of abiding love for God and each other.

The apostle cleverly turns the tables on his physical imprisonment into the imagery of the Spirit's gift when he describes unity as chains of peace. The Ephesians' mentor in the faith is shackled in Roman custody. Effectively the apostle is saying, *Be shackled in God's unifying custody in the chains of peace. Let peace be your bondage.* Peace binds the Christian family together, anchors communal life, and orients the behavior of God's people.

This appeal to peaceful bondage had real consequences for the early Christian community. These were diverse people from diverse cultures trying to get along, trying to make sense of their new identities *in Christ.* This was precisely the apostle's point: unity does not look like mindless, robotic uniformity. It looks like communal submission to one glorious hope for the future. Paul goes on to expound about the diversity of gifts given to the church body. Christ, who is the head of the church, "makes the whole body fit together perfectly. As each part does its own special work, it helps the other parts grow, so that the whole body is healthy and growing and full of love" (Eph. 4:16 NLT).

The appeal to peaceful bondage has real consequences for Christian community today. We are called as diverse people from diverse backgrounds to get along as we seek unity in Christ. We are called to celebrate the different ways we see, hear, taste, touch, and smell the world around us. Uniformity does not make us one, but rather communal submission to the One who weaves us into the beautiful design of missional communities called to be the church in the world. Peace, not obligation or duty or law, chains God's family together in mutual love.

This is the mystery of God's missional church: its unity is defined by its source in God's love. The love of God is expressed in three distinct personalities: parent, child, and spirit. Allowance for variety is woven into the fabric of God's design for unity. The one body bound together in one Spirit has been called to one hope because there is only one Lord, faith, and baptism and one God who permeates every dazzling and diverse drop of creation.

Oneness in Motion

When God's church practices building community together (see chapter 17), the church lives into the unity of the Spirit. Life in community requires a great deal of patience produced not by mere effort but by living lives worthy of God's holy calling. Seeking continually to build community together means honing the skills necessary for sound foundations, solid materials, and sturdy construction. The variety of gifts given to the body by Christ are to "build up the body of Christ, until all of us come to the unity of the faith" (Eph. 4:12 NLT).

When serving compassionately together (see chapter 18), God's church is one. The common ground comes from the humble desire to find ways to express the love and mercy of the Savior. Without the dedicated service of God's people to serve compassionately together, Jesus' ministry of hope and resurrection is rendered effectively crippled. As missional communities find ways to serve the poor, rejected, helpless, and oppressed, God's church is unified around the common cause of God's mission that not one person be excluded from redeeming love.

When worshiping together (see chapter 19), God's church is unified under the banner ascribing love for one Lord who is over all, in all, and through all. The church is not one because it looks the same in every neighborhood and nation, but because the Lord is one and it is into one faith Christ's followers are baptized for one glorious hope. Communal worship must be engaged with humility, gentleness, and patience. The more time God's church spends in worship together, the more the church will reflect the unified love of its source, and the more the church will live in unity.

Unity in Diversity

How do we understand unity if we filter it through the marks of God's missional church? The story of God's church told in Scripture begins with God's people as sent into the entire world to tell all nations about the love of God that results in a holy people united by one God. Filtered by God's mission, unity is the result of God flinging wide the doors of grace to all nations and sending a holy people to live holy lives. Unity is the manifestation of God's people joining God's mission. It is the witness to insiders and outsiders that God is who God says God is, and God loves like God says God will.

> *The church participates in God's mission by proclaiming to the whole world — all classes and cultures, all ages and genders, all nationalities and races — that God is holy love and, through Jesus, God is transforming a people who embody that holy love as empowered and knit together by the Holy Spirit, a sign that the kingdom of God is here.*

God's church is *empowered and knit together by the Holy Spirit,* so it exists as one church, *a sign that the kingdom of God is here.* Diverse communities giving witness to God's love by practicing rhythms that point the way to God are examples of unity. The watching world will know we are Christians by our love, by the distinctive aromas that arise from each branch of God's church, blossoming in the soil of the gospel.

Benediction

> *May the God who is One continue the good work of forming you as one body in Christ so that the world will know Jesus as Savior and Lord through the unity produced by the chains of peace.*
> *Amen.*

Exploration: One Church

❧ Pray the collect together.

❧ Describe a time when you experienced a deep unity with a group of people. What contributed to producing that reality? What emotions do you associate with that experience?

❧ Read Ephesians 4:1–6. What connection do you see between the "bond of peace" and "unity of the Spirit"? What is the source of Christian unity?

❧ Read Ephesians 4:11–16. What contributes to coming to the "unity of the faith"?

❧ Why would those who crafted the Nicene Creed consider oneness as one of the four most important characteristics of the church?

❧ Sometimes we are painfully aware that unity does not come easily. How might making allowance for each other's faults because of your love for one another contribute to unity? What ecclesial practices strengthen the chains of peace God calls us to put on?

❧ Speak the benediction as a blessing to one another and as a call to action in God's mission.

Chapter 17

Partners in the Gospel

Building Community Together

WINTERS IN BLAINE, MINNESOTA, MAKE EVEN THE MOST WARM-blooded person shiver. On Monday and Saturday afternoons, hardy souls make their way to the Manna Market hosted by the SonLight Church. As market workers finish setting up for the 4:45 p.m. opening, guests come in from the cold and visit with their friends.

Manna Market receives perishable foods from local grocers. Rather than just toss out produce near the end of its shelf life, they give the food to Manna Market, which has developed a rapid distribution system for the benefit of families in need. On market days before the shoppers gather, volunteers move the pulpit and Communion Table to reconfigure the worship space. They unload the delivery trucks, sort, and inspect the food. Folding tables line the room set with cardboard boxes and wire baskets that contain the food available that day: vegetables, fruits, dairy products, frozen meat, bread. Foods not appropriate for human consumption go into the compost bin, either for a local pig farmer or to fertilize the community garden on church property used to produce additional foods during the summer.

After someone welcomes the folks and prays for God's blessing, guests fill their shopping bags as they walk past the tables overflowing with food. On the typical day, Manna Market will distribute

10,000 pounds of food. On Sundays the room resounds with praise to God as the congregation sings and prays. On Mondays and Saturdays thanksgiving is expressed for God's provision.

But something else has happened resulting in profound ramifications for much more than just food distribution. A vital community has formed. Most of the volunteers are not members of SonLight Church, but they function with the same *koinonia* described in the New Testament. They come from various parts of the city with family links to different regions of the world. The common ground is their service together at the Manna Market. They know about each other's families. They attend a funeral when death touches the family of a new friend.

Many people consider James as their pastor even though they do not attend SonLight Church. He has heard the confessions of some. When he is out in the community, people he has met at the Manna Market introduce him as "my pastor" to their friends. Children in the fourth grade class at the elementary school recognized him as the pastor of Manna Market when James served as a substitute teacher one day. The congregation that Pastor James serves includes hundreds of people, much greater than the thirty people who regularly attend SonLight Church.

Other congregations support the Manna Market. Roman Catholic, Lutheran, Presbyterian, and non-denominational congregations have contributed thousands of dollars. The wider Christian community has banded together for the sake of the working poor and destitute in Blaine.

SonLight Church remodeled its facility to serve the community better through the Manna Market. Out of their understanding that they form the body of Christ in their community, they made adjustments to enlarge their fellowship. The circle has encompassed other congregations. But most important, it now includes people who at one time lived isolated from their neighbors. This expanded community has not brought numeric growth to SonLight Church, but a whole new expression of the kingdom of God emerged.

Collect

Holy Trinity, Father, Son, and Spirit,
Out of your eternal relationship come grace and love
and fellowship;
Bind our hearts together in love
So that the unity of our fellowship may be a means of
grace to the whole world;
For your sake and for your glory.
Amen.

Embodied Kingdom Values

The apostle Paul recognized that his relationships with others allowed him to enter more fully into the ministry to which he had been called by God. James, Peter, and John (the leaders of the church in Jerusalem) offered the "right hand of fellowship" to Paul and urged him to take the gospel to the Gentiles (Gal. 2:9). Paul rejoiced that he and the congregation in Philippi served together as partners in the gospel (Phil. 1:5). The fellowship of Jesus followers propelled the community toward greater engagement as citizens in God's kingdom.

When the Holy Spirit rushed in on Pentecost, it happened in a social setting. The Holy Spirit, visible as tongues of fire "appeared *among* them" (Acts 2:3, emphasis added). Sometimes we understand the coming of the Holy Spirit at Pentecost in an individualistic manner and miss this communal aspect. James reminded Christians scattered throughout the world that as the church, they formed the "first fruits" in God's harvest (James 1:18). The church reveals the "wisdom of God" (Eph. 3:10). Jesus declared the kingdom of God had begun and the church, filled with the Holy Spirit, stood as a demonstration of that truth.

The preachers in Acts proclaimed the kingdom, not the church. Philip proclaimed the "good news about the kingdom of God and the name of Jesus Christ" (Acts 8:12). When Paul went to Ephesus, for three months he "argued persuasively about the kingdom of God" (Acts 19:8). When Paul arrived in Rome as a prisoner, he spoke to those who visited him from morning until evening, "testifying to the kingdom of God" (Acts 28:23). These early Christian preachers understood the role of the church as bearing witness to the kingdom of God.

The prevenient grace of God puts God way out ahead of the church. The Spirit "blows where it chooses" and is not confined to the structures of the church (John 3:8). The rule and reign of God extends beyond the church and through the Holy Spirit the church forms the corporate body that gives witness to the kingdom.

At SonLight Church some people participate in the Manna Market but are not part of the congregation. They give themselves to a kingdom pattern of living, but they do not acknowledge Jesus as Savior and Lord. In a sense, these people are similar to the man seen casting out demons in Jesus' name. The disciples tried to stop this man since he did not belong to their group. Jesus chastised his overzealous disciples; "Whoever is not against us is for us" (Mark 9:40).

In Paul's discussion of the law, he said that some Gentiles "do instinctively what the law requires" (Rom. 2:14) even though they had not received the written Law as the Jews had. Civil government, Paul said later in his epistle, serves as "God's servant for your good" even if it does not acknowledge its God-given role (Rom. 13:1–4).

Since God uses anyone with values that match the kingdom pattern of living, the church must form solidarity with likeminded groups and persons as together they participate in God's mission. To these people, the church must discern when to speak words of witness to the lordship of Jesus Christ and invite those who live by the kingdom pattern also to acknowledge Jesus as Savior.

To those who acknowledge Jesus as Savior but do not live by the kingdom pattern, the church must continually challenge persons to a whole-life discipleship. James said that "faith by itself, if it has no works, is dead" (James 2:17). Both are needed to be the church: to acknowledge Jesus as Savior and Lord and to live by the kingdom pattern.

Companions: *With-Bread* People

Important events in Jesus' life revealed the gospel in the context of a meal. One time Jesus had dinner at the house of a Pharisee. As he reclined at the table, a sinful woman washed Jesus' feet with her tears, much to the dismay of his host. People like this woman who had been marginalized by religious standards found a welcome through a relationship with the reigning King.

On another day the disciples directed Jesus to escape the crowds by going to Bethsaida, but the throng discovered where Jesus had gone and followed. Late in the afternoon, while he taught the people about the kingdom of God and in response to the disciples' concern, Jesus fed the multitude with five loaves of bread and two fish. God cares for the physical needs of people.

Jesus explained the atonement at a Passover meal with his disciples. At a table in a home in Emmaus, two disciples recognized the resurrected Lord, then hurried to tell the other disciples the good news. Good things happen at a meal.

Just as was true in Jesus' life, so for us as well the sharing of a meal often involves more than physical sustenance. The word *companion* is derived from a Latin compound (*com-* + *panis*, "with" + "bread"). A companion is literally a "bread fellow." The word communion is compounded as well (*com-* + *unus*, "with" + "union" or "oneness"). Community, then, is when people share or participate in unity.

From the beginning of the church, followers of Jesus have revealed the gospel as "they broke bread at home and ate their food with glad and generous hearts" (Acts 2:46). Sometimes jokes are made about the church and potlucks, and some very humorous stories can be told about congregational dinners. Looking at the issue of building community, however, eating together may be one of the best things a group can do.

Some congregations urge their members to join other congregational members in a shared meal during the week for the sake of strengthening relationships. Other congregational leaders challenge people to intentionally seek opportunities to share meals with those beyond the congregation. Through these intentional ecclesial practices, they build community as they "share bread."

Grace Evangelical Church deliberately enlarged its community when it started partnering with area helping agencies. In his desire for the people of his congregation to engage more fully in ministry to the people of St. Joseph, Missouri, Pastor Darrell visited organizations doing work that fit the kingdom pattern. Rather than trying to recreate a church version of the various services, Darrell met and established partnerships with groups already serving the broader community. The Hands of Grace ministry now partners with twenty-three helping agencies to assist individuals and families in northwest Missouri. Some members of the congregation volunteer each week; others join the monthly service project. In all instances they link arms in solidarity to employ better the kingdom pattern of living.

In too many instances, a congregation's attempts to foster the fellowship have been divorced from the church's mission. A men's fishing trip and a women's craft night will build community, but mostly in an inward-focused manner. The camaraderie that develops on a short-term mission trip, for example, builds community too, but does so as the group participates in God's mission together. Rather than planning fellowship events with the hope that out of the nurtured relationships something missional will occur, God's mission would be better served if the missional community committed to align itself to God's mission through rigorous engagement. They would see a robust sense of community naturally grow out of their mission together.

Broaden the Community

Just as Paul recognized his partnership with others in his missionary endeavors, so leaders of missional communities today know that they must build a deep sense of community to engage fully in God's mission. Missional living is a team endeavor. Community development comes within a congregation as its members care for one another, bear each other's burdens, and encourage one another.

When people work together out of a genuine love for each other, it magnifies their effectiveness as missionaries.

But as the story of SonLight Church shows, a missional community will enlarge its borders to include all who lean into the kingdom pattern. The apostolic impulse of the church calls for the catholic inclusion of all who follow Jesus no matter the denominational tradition. The commitment to put God's kingdom as the ultimate endeavor will prompt solidarity with all who exemplify the kingdom pattern. In doing so, *koinonia* demonstrates to the world that the kingdom of God is at hand.

Benediction

May the Triune God knit your hearts together as
one so that the world will know the love of God,
the forgiveness of the Savior, and hope through the
abiding presence of the Holy Spirit.
Amen.

Exploration: Building Community Together

❧ Pray the collect together.

❧ People involved in the Manna Market talk about how they feel a sense of community they did not have before. Describe the difference between feeling isolated and feeling part of something bigger than yourself.

❧ Read Philippians 1:3–11. We have an image of Paul as being a man with tremendous ability. What does it say, then, when he acknowledges how important the community of Jesus followers was in his ministry?

❧ Since the church is to proclaim the kingdom of God and not itself, what adjustments might need to be made to align better with God's mission in this regard?

❧ What are some "with bread" moments in the life of your missional community? How might those times be enhanced so as to strengthen the mission?

❧ Identify relationships between your missional community and others in the broader community that live into the kingdom pattern. What new relationships might "provoke [all parties involved] to love and good deeds" (Heb. 10:24)?

❧ Speak the benediction as a blessing to one another and as a call to action in God's mission.

Chapter 18

Whatever Love Demands

Serving Compassionately Together

THE SMELL OF FRESHLY PREPARED FOOD EMANATED FROM THE kitchen. Dining tables dotted the worship space. Artists arranged their face paint and brushes. Workers erected bounce houses. Containers of backpacks, crayons, pencils, paper, scissors, and glue were meticulously organized and displayed. Volunteers, young and old, could be seen darting around the building making last-minute preparations, each one of them wearing a bright orange shirt that simply read "here to serve." This was no typical Wednesday night at Springfield Church.

Weeks before, the congregation's leadership team mulled over the idea of hosting a Back-to-School Bash, an event that they hoped would reach out and touch a need in their community. With the economic recession hitting pockets of their city especially hard and autumn approaching, they knew the need for basic school supplies was great for several families in their community. *But will anyone show up?*

Springfield Church had been in decline for decades. The primary mission had become survival. They had never hosted an event like this before. Many in leadership had stopped believing that God could really use them to make a difference. The congregation made some basic modifications to their building with new persons in mind. Pastor Brandin focused his preaching for weeks on the mission of God as the primary reason for the church's existence. These things served to help awaken the congregation to the missional call of God.

But nothing would prepare them for the dramatic transformation that would come as a result of serving their community together on that late summer evening.

An hour before the doors were scheduled to open, a long line had already formed in front of the building. When the event officially started, the facility was flooded with hundreds of people from the community, most of whom had never stepped foot in the church building before. The backpacks the congregation had prepared were claimed quickly and the additional supplies were going fast. Volunteers scrambled to take down names and phone numbers for rain checks, informing people that if they were able to come up with more supplies, they would be contacted.

The air was electric with excitement as the space filled with new faces. Congregational members and guests shared a meal together. New friendships, bonds, and community partnerships formed. Neighborhood children received essential items they needed to begin their school year well. This congregation, which had quietly existed for years, was now known as the church that serves.

People soon realized that a crowd was not the only thing that entered the church building that night. A fresh breath of the Spirit had blown through a once-dying community.

The following Sunday morning the congregation spent the majority of the worship service celebrating what God had done. They exuberantly shared testimonies about the evening's experience and the congregation as a whole sensed what it meant to be born again.

The people of Springfield Church keenly recognized that something unique had taken place on the property, unlike any outreach efforts they had attempted before. Their building became more than a meeting place for the faithful. It now served as a mission outpost for the sent. The heart of this congregation had been revived and now pulsated with renewed passion for the mission of God.

Collect

Servant King,
Who took up the towel and basin to wash the feet of
humanity;
Teach us to take the posture of humble service
So that your love may be known in all the world;
For the glory and praise of God.
Amen.

Self-emptying Love

One of the earliest and most well-known Christian hymns in Scripture is often referred to as the kenosis hymn from the Greek word *ekenosen*, "he emptied." It calls the church to have the same mind as Christ Jesus, "who, though he was in the form of God, did not regard equality with God as something to be exploited, but emptied himself, taking the form of a slave" (Phil. 2:6–7). The hymn reveals the manner in which the people of God are called to live out God's mission. In Philippians and other letters, Paul saw himself as a servant of Christ and envisioned the church to be a servant community, shaped by the pattern and life of its Lord.

In one of the most stirring scenes in the Gospels, Jesus literally took the position of a slave as he washed the feet of his disciples around the Passover table. He taught his followers by saying, "I have set you an example, that you also should do as I have done to you" (John 13:15). This action is remarkable in its own right, but is intensified when we realize that Jesus even washed the feet of Judas, his betrayer.

The call to serve does not diminish in the presence of danger, persecution, or opposition. In fact, it is precisely in these moments when the necessity for self-emptying love is needed most. Any service the church engages in is not offered simply to like-minded organizations or to those who can repay it. Nor is service done for the sake of the praise and attention of others. In the kingdom of

God, there is no place for triumphalism or arrogance. The church is called to take the same posture as its humble Lord, emptying itself of all but love.

One day when Jesus was leaving the city of Jericho, two blind men on the side of the road cried out to him for mercy. "Moved with compassion, Jesus touched their eyes. Immediately they regained their sight and followed him" (Matt. 20:34). Compassion led Jesus to meet real tangible human needs with the resources of God. These acts of service were not a side project for Jesus, a temporary distraction from his busy schedule of preaching the word. They were integral to his mission. "For the Son of Man came not to be served but to serve, and to give his life a ransom for many" (Mark 10:45). In the same way, service is not just one activity of the church but an ongoing posture of the body of Christ in the world.

The church draws from the example and the promise of Christ. Jesus made the bold claim that "the one who believes in me will also do the works that I do and, in fact, will do greater works than these" (John 14:12). As the church trusts in its living Lord, it can walk confidently in the power of the Spirit to continue the loving service that Jesus embodied in the world.

When Jesus healed the sick, gave sight to the blind, and fed the hungry, these served as signs that the kingdom of God had arrived. In the same way, when the church has compassion (*com-* + *pati*, "together" + "suffer") for a broken world and is moved to act, the church functions as a beautiful testimony to the in-breaking of God's kingdom. Compassion is the motivation for service. Humility is the means. Gifted by the Spirit of God, the church is called to bear witness to the reign of God through compassionate, humble acts of love.

Sustained Service

Jesus came announcing the arrival of the kingdom of God. He was anointed and sent to "proclaim the year of the Lord's favor" (Luke 4:19). His proclamation quickened the hearts and minds of his hearers and led them to repent and enter new life in the kingdom. But the ministry of Jesus was more than just words—it took on flesh (John 1:14). Jesus proclaimed the kingdom but also demonstrated it with his Spirit-empowered actions.

The church lives and ministers in a world where talk is cheap. Words that are not accompanied by deeds will most certainly fall on deaf ears. The culture is, by and large, disillusioned with those in positions of authority who are quick to make sweeping claims and promises but slow to follow through.

There is an increasing awareness that mission should be less an occasional project we accomplish here and there and more an ongoing engagement with the needs of our world. This kind of service is challenging, requiring long-term investment, and, more importantly, the cultivation of relationships. Apart from our dependence on the power of the Holy Spirit and a deep spirituality, this kind of sustained service cannot be accomplished.

When a missional community chooses to step forward in service, the attitude with which it serves is as important as the service itself. Too often the church has entered a situation with an attempt to fix things, thus diminishing the dignity of those it has come to serve. Other times the church serves but does so with unspoken expectations or hidden agendas. There are times when the church has overpromised and under delivered, resulting in frustration and mistrust. The challenge for the church in our day is to serve in a way that is humble, consistent, and sensitive to those who find themselves in need. To do so effectively means we must serve with the goal to listen and learn as much as we speak and act; to receive as much as we give.

Many congregations have strategies to help connect people to service opportunities that serve the life of the congregation. This is healthy and biblical. However, these efforts can sometimes stop short of including ministries that reach outside the walls of the church building. While there is a need for church-based ministries to address particular needs, more and more missional communities are finding value in looking beyond the congregation to find partners who are willing to work for the common good.

For instance, Springfield Church invited several professional hairdressers from their city to participate in the Back-to-School

Bash. These men and women, most of whom had no church connection but loved the idea of serving, shared their gifts with the underserved children in their community. Partnership and collaboration for the sake of God's mission can often open doors to service that otherwise may not have existed.

Other communities regularly collaborate with existing nonprofit organizations and equip and encourage their members to serve within them on a regular basis. Furthermore, they are looking at their congregation's level of engagement with these opportunities as a barometer of church health.

Many vibrant missional communities have started by asking the question, *What is God doing in our midst?* They have taken the time to research what needs surround them, who is already working to address those needs, and how to engage strategically and prayerfully. Other times God suddenly brings an unexpected need to the attention of the community and a missional community must be attentive enough and nimble to respond appropriately. The corporate practice of discernment (see chapter 5) is essential in helping communities know how and when to serve.

Transformed by Serving

"We had been dead for so long, but now we were alive." This is how Brandin described the transformation that came to his congregation when they chose to serve their community. Following the initial event, the congregation began hosting a free garage sale and a Mother's Day banquet for single moms. They also developed a relationship with their local school to provide the playground with a much needed update. All of these initiatives have now become ongoing efforts to serve the needs of their neighborhood. Community partnerships have multiplied in the process.

When believers engage in compassionate service together, it not only affects the lives of those being served. It can change the trajectory of an entire faith community. Service builds connection within the body and provides the opportunity to serve Christ himself (Matt. 25:40).

Benediction

May Jesus, who stooped to wash his disciples' feet,
use your compassionate service so that the world will
know the healing touch of God.
Amen.

Exploration: Serving Compassionately Together

❧ Pray the collect together.

❧ Describe a personal experience similar to the service provided to the community through the Back-to-School Bash. What emotions might the recipients have felt? Those who served?

❧ Read Matthew 20:29–34. Describe the crowd's response to the blind men. Contrast the crowd with Jesus' response. What did the two blind men do after they were healed?

❧ What role did service play in the life and ministry of Jesus? Was it a means to an end or an end in itself?

❧ As you think about your missional community, describe current forms of compassionate service.

❧ List some needs your broader community or neighborhood is facing. Have each member select one to research and bring a report back to the group. Decide as a missional community how you will live out your faith in compassionate service.

❧ Speak the benediction as a blessing to one another and as a call to action in God's mission.

Chapter 19

Service to God

Worshiping Together

ERIC KNELT DOWN, HIS HEAD BOWED. *I BAPTIZE YOU IN THE NAME OF the Father, and of the Son, and of the Holy Spirit.* The words spoken over him rang out as the water flowed over his head and filled the font below. Eric's wife and children stood nearby, giving testimony to the work of God's grace in his life.

Gathered around to celebrate with Eric were members of Eden Community that had recently been planted in Portland, Oregon. While Eric had not always been open to the idea of church and was at times staunchly against it, God was doing something new in his life through this worshiping community.

The events leading up to this moment started a few weeks before when after an Easter Sunday gathering, Eric had come up to Pastor Jason and motioned toward his heart saying, "Jason, something is happening in here." Eric went on to explain that seeing the Easter baptisms that day had spoken to him at a deep level in a way he'd never experienced before. He told of his desire to follow Christ and be an example for his wife and children.

Almost a year after his baptism, Eric again approached Jason. "I'm not a public speaker, but I need to tell others about what has happened to me." The following week, as Jason was preaching on Paul's conversion (Acts 9), Eric stood before the community and shared his powerful story of transformation.

For Eden Community, worship is the heartbeat of life and mission together. Eden views their weekly gatherings of worship as the time when missionaries who have been sent out come together to celebrate what God is doing in their midst. This community believes that without worship there can be no mission. They also believe that mission that does not lead to worship is incomplete.

Portland is one of the least religious cities in the United States and megachurches are rare. For many that have no former Christian memory or experience, a traditional worship service on Sunday morning represents a foreign culture. Therefore, Eden Community meets on Sunday nights in a café space and seeks to encourage and equip believers while also creating an environment that is welcoming to spiritual seekers.

The key for Eden is to keep worship uncompromisingly God-centered. They use a variety of expressions to help worshipers focus on the gospel of Christ. Some elements are ancient and rooted in Scripture and tradition, reflective of the universal church. Others are fresh and organic, reflecting the language and style of Portland's culture.

The Scriptures saturate each gathering with the sacrament of Communion central. The arts play a strong role and interactivity in worship for all ages is highly valued both in liturgy and in planning. Through their weekly gatherings, Eden Community seeks to be immersed in the story of God so they can embody that story as they are sent out in mission.

Collect

> *God of grace,*
> *Who bathes creation with your holy presence;*
> *Help us to worship in spirit and in truth*
> *So that the praise of our lips matches the tenor of our*
> *lives;*
> *In the name of Jesus Christ, our lofty example.*
> *Amen.*

To *Be* God's Praise

A woman once told a Bible teacher that she did not fully understand the apocalyptic message of the book of Revelation, but upon reading it carefully she was moved to worship God. The teacher responded, "You have grasped the message of this book."

The imagery is powerful: "There was a great multitude that no one could count, from every nation, from all tribes and peoples and languages, standing before the throne and before the Lamb, robed in white, with palm branches in their hands. They cried out in a loud voice, saying, 'Salvation belongs to our God who is seated on the throne, and to the Lamb!'" (Rev. 7:9–10).

According to Revelation, the reign of God consists of a healed and reconciled community joining together with all creation in shouts of praise and adoration. The purposes of God are celebrated as heaven and earth are renewed and Christ is enthroned as Lord of all. Everyone acknowledges the living God as the source of light and life. There is a beautiful and diverse tapestry of human culture and language, yet one voice and song resounds, praising the crucified and risen Lamb.

But it is more than just a song. The lives of the worshipers have been transformed. Those who stand to sing "have come out of the great ordeal; they have washed their robes and made them white in the blood of the Lamb" (Rev. 7:14). Redeemed people who relentlessly pursue the glory of God inhabit God's new world. There is no place for injustice or unrighteousness. Divine love pervades all of creation and God is pleased to dwell among God's people in peace.

This heavenly vision of worship serves as a pattern for the church as we pray and work for God's kingdom to come on earth as it is in heaven. The ultimate goal of mission is that "every knee should bend, in heaven and on earth and under the earth, and every tongue should confess that Jesus Christ is Lord, to the glory of God the Father" (Phil. 2:10–11). Worship is most fully expressed when a community is devoted to the lordship of Christ and the confession of the mouth is authenticated by the integrity of heart and life.

Worship is not a monologue. Rather, when a community gathers, God speaks and God's people respond. Each encounter establishes and renews the covenant relationship between God and God's people through song, gesture, and symbol. Heaven invades earth as God's people are caught up in the glory and majesty of God.

God uses the practice of gathered worship as a means of transforming communities into the reflection of God's glory for the sake of the world. The early Christians came together "on the first day of the week" (Acts 20:7) to encounter the risen Christ in word, song, and sacrament. Here they confessed their faith, heard from and discussed the Scriptures, encouraged one another, shared the Lord's Supper, and gave of their means for the needs of the community. This rhythm in their gatherings fueled them for mission.

Missional worship will be unapologetically focused on Christ. It will be diverse, reflecting the various cultures where communities are found. And it will send the people out, transformed by its encounter with God, to be the body of Christ in the world.

Participating in God's Story

Missional communities work diligently to welcome people at all stages of spiritual maturity into meaningful expressions of worship. They will utilize the language of joy, sorrow, doubt, and belief. Missional communities believe that when God is exalted in meaningful, contextual, and hospitable worship, seekers will be drawn to Christ by the power of the Spirit. Many congregations keep their worship God-centered by following the Christian calendar. This orders the congregation's life and liturgy around the person of Jesus Christ and connects worshipers with the church universal.

A missional community's worship is not a presentation people come to watch. Instead, it is an invitation for the whole community to participate in the story of God's saving work through acts that engage the heart, mind, and body. Christ is present in the gathered community through word, song, sign, and symbol. Interaction is highly valued as worshipers serve as a means of grace to each other.

The recovery of the use of the ancient creeds helps connect disciples of Jesus with the church throughout history. The sacraments are being recovered as visible sermons that demonstrate the power of the gospel. Numerous communities are exploring ways to engage all of the senses in worship by recovering ancient forms and creating new ones.

Missional worship is not limited to a particular style; rather, it is concerned with faithfully proclaiming the gospel in the language and metaphors of the culture in which it occurs. A North American teacher once traveled to Africa to speak at a conference. He could hardly contain his excitement to experience another culture's worship but was soon dismayed when the group immediately began singing an imported, Western Christian pop song. These Christians did not sing in their *heart* language.

Songs and prayers of other cultures can help emphasize the universality of the church, but we must not neglect the call to contextualize for our own time and place. In an effort to help the worship truly become the people's work, many congregations employ the use of a team that gathers and creates prayers, songs, and visual media for use in worship.

Missional communities will embrace the voices of various generations in their worship planning and leading, as the passing along of the faith is critical to the process of making disciples. The variety of generations serves to enrich the life of the community and illustrates the unity of the church.

Worship can help people enter into the narrative of Scripture and connect it with God's mission in the present. One congregation highlighted this connection on Palm Sunday. Just as Christ rode into Jerusalem and the people laid their garments on the road to welcome him (Mark 11:8), the community was invited to bring forward donated clothing that were then given to those in need. This illustrates the fact that missional God-centered worship will always propel a community outward in mission to the world.

Holistic Worship

One Sunday, instead of meeting in their normal location, Eden Community's worship gathering took place in a run-down building in east Portland. Instead of instruments or Bibles, worshipers held paintbrushes, shovels, and rakes. That day, members of Eden Community cleaned and painted a building that would be used to serve at-risk youth in the neighborhood. Just before they began the work, they prayed together that God would receive the service done as an act of worship.

For some congregations, a worship service is only considered an event where people come to receive. Much effort is made to ensure that worshipers have a good experience. But a missional community understands worship primarily as the church's offering of itself in service *to* God. When this posture is taken, gatherings of worship serve to shape the whole church's life into one that exhibits passionate love for God and neighbor.

Benediction

May God, who bathes creation with a holy presence,
make you a pleasing offering to God so that your
very being will fill the world with the sweet aroma of
Christ.
Amen.

Exploration: Worshiping Together

❧ Pray the collect together.

❧ Describe a moment in worship when you especially sensed God's presence. How did that experience affect your congregation?

❧ Read Isaiah 6:1–8. How did this encounter affect the prophet Isaiah personally? What effect did it have on his ministry?

❧ Why are we tempted to make worship about us? In what ways is this sometimes expressed in the church?

❧ Reflect on your community's gatherings. What changes might make them more God-centered? Hospitable? Diverse?

❧ Write a list of common elements or roles in your community's gatherings. Next to each one, list the names of people in your community who have gifts to contribute but are not currently involved.

❧ Speak the benediction as a blessing to one another and as a call to action in God's mission.

Notes

Chapter 1

[1] John Wesley, "Sermon 16: The Means of Grace," in *Wesley's 52 Standard Sermons*, (Salem, Ohio: H. E. Schmul, 1967), 149–162.

Chapter 2

[1] See Graham Hughes, *Worship as Meaning: A Liturgical Theology for Late Modernity*, Part II (New York: Cambridge University Press, 2003) and Clayton J. Schmit, *Sent and Gathered: A Worship Manual for the Missional Church* (Grand Rapids, Michigan: Baker Academic, 2009), 108–117, for discussions of Charles Peirce and semiotics.

[2] Crystal L. Downing, *Changing Signs of Truth: A Christian Introduction to the Semiotics of Communication* (Downers Grove, Illinois: IVP Academic, 2012), 22ff.

[3] Tim Suttle, "How to Shrink Your Church," *The Huffington Post*, accessed January 11, 2014, *www.huffingtonpost.com/tim-suttle/how-to-shrink-your-church_b_1095841.html*.

[4] *Ibid.*

[5] To read the full discussion of these ideas, see Tim Suttle, *Shrink: Faithful Ministry in a Church-Growth Culture* (Grand Rapids, Michigan: Zondervan, 2014).

[6] "Redemption Church: Our Story," accessed January 11, 2014, *redemptionchurchkc.com/ourstory*.

Chapter 3

[1] Charles Van Engen, *God's Missionary People: Rethinking the Purpose of the Local Church* (Grand Rapids, Michigan: Baker Academic, 1991), 68.

[2] Darrell L. Guder, ed., *Missional Church: A Vision for the Sending of the Church in North America* (Grand Rapids, Michigan: Eerdmans, 1998), 254–264.

[3] Emil Brunner, *The Word and the World* (London: Student Christian Movement Press, 1931), 108.

Chapter 6
[1] Barbara Brown Taylor, *An Altar in the World: A Geography of Faith* (New York: Harper One, 2009), 179.
[2] Libby Tedder, "Prayer and our Relationship with God," in *Relational Theology: A Contemporary Introduction*, ed. Brint Montgomery et al. (Eugene, Oregon: Wipf & Stock, 2012), 68–69.

Chapter 7
[1] Henri J. M. Nouwen, *Reaching Out: The Three Movements of the Spiritual Life* (New York: Doubleday, 1975), 51.

Chapter 11
[1] Desmond Tutu, *God is Not a Christian and Other Provocations* (New York: Harper One, 2011), xii.

Chapter 16
[1] "Global Christianity: A Report on the Size and Distribution of the World's Christian Population," The Pew Forum on Religion and Public Life, accessed April 20, 2013, *www.pewforum.org/ Christian/Global-Christianity-worlds-christian-population.aspx*.

Missional Communities

Chapter 2
Redemption Church (www.redemptionchurchkc.com) is a missional community in Olathe, Kansas. Tim Suttle is a founding pastor. Tim writes for *The Huffington Post* (www.huffingtonpost.com/tim-suttle) and is an active blogger (www.patheos.com/blogs/paperbacktheology).

Chapter 5
The Open Door (www.pghopendoor.org) is a missional community in Pittsburgh's East End. The Garfield Community Farm (www.garfieldfarm.com) was started by The Open Door community in partnership with the Valley View Presbyterian Church. BJ Woodworth and John Creasy serve as pastors of The Open Door.

Chapter 6
The Care House (www.nfcnaz.org/ministries/care-house) is a ministry of the First Church of the Nazarene in Nampa, Idaho. Monica Miller manages the ministry of The Care House. James Austin is on the pastoral staff at Nampa First.

Chapter 7
The Canaan Hill Church of the Nazarene is located in Lawson, Missouri. Jim Swindell is a licensed minister who serves as part of the leadership team for ministry among those who live at HideAway Lakes. John Ramsey, Carissa Ramsey, and Michael Falgout serve as the pastoral team at Canaan Hill Church.

Chapter 9
The opening story occurred at the First Church of the Nazarene (www.lowellfirstchurch.org) in Lowell, Massachusetts, where John

Megyesi serves as pastor. Jeff Lane is now the pastor of the Urban Promise Church of Somerville, Massachusetts. Jeff is the co-author of *The Samaritan Project*. Kelley Lane is the executive director of Sibling Connections (www.siblingconnections.org), an organization that facilitates the reunion of brothers and sisters separated by foster care placement. Joanne Bastien is a supervisor with the Massachusetts Department of Children and Families.

Discovery Church of the Nazarene (www.discovery-livermore. com) is located in Livermore, California. Curtis Lillie leads the congregation as pastor.

Chapter 10
New Beginnings Church of the Nazarene (www.newbeginnings-church.tv) is in Lee's Summit, Missouri. Shane Ash serves as a pastor at New Beginnings. See his blog (www.shaneash.com) for more on the congregation's journey.

Chapter 11
Clear Creek Church (www.clearcreekpdx.com) is in Gresham, Oregon. Gary Tribbett serves as a pastor at Clear Creek and the president of Compassion Connect (www.compassionconnect.com), a non-profit organization that mobilizes congregations to compassionately serve in the Portland metropolitan area and other world regions. Linda Tribbett is a director of Adorned in Grace (www.adornedingrace.org), a ministry that functions under the Compassion Connect umbrella.

Chapter 13
Hillside Church of the Nazarene (www.petalumahillsidechurch. com) is located in Petaluma, California, where Brad Edgbert served as the pastor. Brad recently moved to plant a new missional community in Olympia, Washington. Bart and Sandi Johnson help lead the compassionate service to those living in the tent community.

Chapter 14
Common Cathedral (www.ecclesia-ministries.org/common_cathedral.html) is a program of Ecclesia Ministries that serves the

chronically un-housed adults in downtown Boston. Deborah Little refers to herself as a street priest (www.ecclesia-ministries.org/ecclesia/journey_to_priest.html) and was ordained by The Episcopal Church.

Chapter 15
The healing choir is a ministry of the Bethel Church of the Nazarene in Quincy, Massachusetts, led by Pastor Jeff Barker. Sean Coleman facilitates the ministry of the healing choir.

Chapter 17
SonLight Church of the Nazarene (www.sonlightnaz.org) is located in Blaine, Minnesota. James Chapman serves as the pastor. Information on the Manna Market and the community garden is available at the congregation's website (www.sonlightnaz.org/mannamarket.html).

Grace Evangelical Church (www.graceontheweb.org) in St. Joseph, Missouri, is led by Pastor Darrell Jones.

Chapter 18
Pastor Brandin Melton leads the First Church of the Nazarene (www.sfnchurch.com) in Springfield, Missouri.

Chapter 19
Eden Community (www.edenpdx.org) is a missional community in Portland, Oregon, where Jason Veach serves as the founding pastor. Eden Community was planted as a parent-affiliated congregation of Portland First Church of the Nazarene (www.pfcn.org) led by Pastor Mark Goodwin.

Authors

LIBBY TEDDER HUGUS is planting a missional community in Casper, Wyoming. She has contributed chapters to *Love Among Us, Relational Theology: A Contemporary Introduction, One in Christ: Reconciliation, Justice, and Mutuality,* and *Conversations on Holiness.* Libby drafted chapters 4, 6, 8, 11, 12, and 16.

KEITH SCHWANZ has served as a pastor, church musician, and seminary educator. He is the founder of Storian Press. Keith wrote *The Birth of a Hymn,* edited *Missio Dei: A Wesleyan Understanding* and *One in Christ: Reconciliation, Justice, and Mutuality,* and contributed to *Postmodern and Wesleyan?: Exploring the Boundaries and Possibilities.* Keith drafted chapters 1, 2, 3, 7, 10, 15, and 17.

JASON VEACH serves as the pastor of Eden Community, a missional community in Portland, Oregon. He has served in pastoral ministry in Kansas and as a chapel supervisor and lecturer at European Nazarene College in Büsingen, Germany. He contributed to *One in Christ: Reconciliation, Justice, and Mutuality.* Jason drafted chapters 5, 9, 13, 14, 18, and 19.

ONE IN CHRIST

Reconciliation, Justice, and Mutuality

FOREWORD BY RON BENEFIEL

KEITH SCHWANZ, EDITOR

see the five-star reviews on amazon.com

Contents

Description

Paul had good news for the church in Galatia: "There is no longer Jew or Greek ... slave or free ... male and female; for all of you are one in Christ Jesus" (Gal. 3:28). Their Christian unity prevailed over the issues that previously created roadblocks in their relationships. Distinctions of race, culture, socioeconomic status, and gender faded in the bright reality of their faith in Jesus as Savior and Lord.

Just as Paul urge the early Christians to reveal their faith through their actions, so God calls the church to live out the good news for the sake of the world in the twenty-first century.

- Reconciliation—to settle differences
- Justice—to treat fairly
- Mutuality—to share equally

As the church embodies these qualities, God brings healing to strained relationships, equality to biased relationships, and parity to imbalanced relationships. This is good news for everyone in any era.

Excerpt from Chapter 1

At the heart of Charles Dickens's classic *A Christmas Carol* is a confrontation between the miserly Ebenezer Scrooge and his late business partner, Jacob Marley. Scrooge is a shrewd businessman, and for him the value of a person related directly to that person's material success. Marley, however, had suffered after death because of that very perspective, and he was trying desperately to reshape his old friend's distorted values.

The following dialogue captures the essence of Marley's concern for Scrooge:

"But you were always a good man of business, Jacob," faltered Scrooge, who now began to apply this to himself.

"Business!" cried the Ghost, wringing its hands again. "Mankind [*sic*] was my business. The common welfare was my business; charity, mercy, forbearance, and benevolence were all my business. The dealings of my trade were but a drop of water in the comprehensive ocean of my business!"

At the time Dickens was writing, the whole of his native England professed to be Christian. Yet, as Dickens made clear in most of his stories, very few of the wealthy and powerful in his culture would have agreed with Marley. And I suspect that even in our time Dickens's concerns continue to resonate.

But what of the Christian church? Do we live and think and preach and write as though humankind is our business? The difficulty with this for people who are deeply religious is that religion sometimes seems *intended* to draw distinctions that exclude some people. Isn't religion essentially about determining who is in and who is out; who is saved and who is condemned; who is good and who is bad? In some ways, perhaps, this description might be defensible. But as Christians we must insist that division is not the heart of the good news of Christianity.

The good news of Jesus Christ is not for a specific kind of person, or for a person of a certain social status, or for a person of a particular gender or race. The good news of Jesus Christ is for all people irrespective of the categories and qualities that normally divide us. The gospel is not a message intended to push people away. The gospel of Jesus intends to draw people both toward the God who created them and toward each other. It is a message of healed relationships, of forgiveness for harms done, of justice and equality for all people, of selflessness and the sharing of blessings and resources.

CPSIA information can be obtained at www.ICGtesting.com
Printed in the USA
LVOW12s1123060814

397817LV00011B/144/P